CW00507185

GIRLS & BOYS

GIRLS & BOYS

THE LIMITS OF
NON-SEXIST
CHILDREARING

Sara Stein

CHATTO & WINDUS

THE HOGARTH PRESS

LONDON

Published in 1984 by
Chatto & Windus · The Hogarth Press
40 William IV Street
London WC2N 4DF

British Library Cataloguing in Publication Data

Stein, Sara
   Girls and boys.
   1. Sex role in children
   I. Title
   305.2′3   BF723.S42
   ISBN 0–7011–2887–9
   ISBN 0–7011–2888–7 Pbk

Printed in Great Britain by
Redwood Burn
Trowbridge, Wiltshire

For Marty

CONTENTS

PREFACE

When I was ten, I was a tomboy. I thought most girls were prissy, silly things, which was what the boys I biked with thought. When I grew up and married, I wished only for baby boys and, indeed, had four of them. They were a great compensation for having been born a girl myself. I can remember comparing muscles with them, handling the snakes they brought home with real enthusiasm, sharing their boisterous fun. Then how could it be, as the youngest approached adolescence, that I yearned to have a daughter?

That is how this book began. Some resistance to being womanly and to taking pleasure in girlishness began to loosen. As the strictures fell away, I realized they had never been altogether comfortable. Memories awoke—of my mother, whose silver-topped jars of creams and powders had once delighted me and with whom long soaks in a hot tub and inviting cuddle times in her large bed were now palpable. The rough smell of my father's tweed coat on a winter day once more filled my nostrils. He gave me a silk kimono—the pale chrysanthemums reappeared—and a garnet ring. Those times preceded the years of overalls. I had changed then; I was changing again.

There was a sturdy bridge between the bulkhead of my earliest memories, when perfume had seemed worth waiting for, and the present when, out of the blue, I asked my husband to buy me a tiny bottle of Joy. The bridge had nothing to do with the fact that I remained a fiend at clearing woodland. I long for a daughter—daughter-in-law, granddaughter—because I am not only female by a once disparaged accident of fate, but feminine at my very core, where mother and daughter are in some sense the same, and welcome being so.

Then what was the difference between the tomboy that spanned those times and a genuine boy? That is the subject of this book—the real kernel of masculinity and femininity, how each comes about, sustains itself, and expresses itself over years, and why that kernel is so important.

Answers have come to me from many sources. An abiding interest in biology led me to the work of animal behaviorists and anthropologists who determinedly probe behavior of all sorts to see how it is related to the exigencies of living. Feminist writings were helpful on two scores: for their resolute insistence that we have failed to tap the riches of either sex and for their irresolution on the many conflicts that plague women's liberation and nonsexist childrearing. On the subject of child development itself, I have to thank scores of psychologists whose patient work has revealed many strands in the complicated texture of childhood. I am particularly grateful for the work of Margaret Mahler, a psychoanalyst who has teased apart the knottiest portions of all. And I could not have done without Edward Walsh, who searched the literature and culled and organized it for me. The writings that were most helpful and may be enjoyed by readers are listed in the bibliography.

My deepest thanks belong to my family—to my mother, who stuck to her preference for red velvet party dresses; to my father, who entertained my boyish pretensions with the compromise of sharing his gardens with me; and to my sons, who, as they take on their own brand of adulthood, kindly accentuate their differences.

Most of all I thank my husband, Marty. To both of us, the importance of being masculine or feminine had for years been a mystery whose elusiveness was matched only by the unlikable prospect of having to find out too much about it. The need to find out was spurred by those newly vivid recollections of childhood, but that was only half my life. The other half has been lived with Marty, whose strength of purpose in first suggesting that I write about this subject, and whose help in unraveling it, has made it possible for me to follow the growth of masculinity and femininity to surprisingly likable conclusions.

Pound Ridge, New York
July 1983

GIRLS & BOYS

1

NOT QUITE FREE

The bold experiment to raise nonsexist children is not working. Boys are not dressing baby dolls. Girls are not playing with trucks. This problem is baffling those who have devoted themselves to eradicating sexism and sex stereotypes in their families. "The most important thing you can do," claims one woman executive, "is to change your own role models. Sometimes my husband cooks, sometimes I do; sometimes he fixes the toys, sometimes I do. We each are careful to spend a great deal of time alone with the children, and we both work less than full time in order to be home with them. But when my son came to visit my office, it took hours to convince him that my staff worked for me and not for Daddy."

Jenny, whose mother is a doctor, believes only boys can be doctors. She plays at being a nurse. Sarah's parents are both full-time professionals. When she grows up, she plans to be a bride, or maybe a princess. Four-year-old Ned explains what men are like: They build houses, they are the boss and the president. Why can't women build houses? "Because," Ned explains, "they know they can't do that hard work, they know if they were working, like on a building, they might think a man might get stuck in the thing or something like that." A man can be president because "he knows what to do on time." A woman can't be president because "she does not get as smart as a man."

How come Jerry, who has heard only nonsexist stories, himself relates tales of risk, collision, and disaster—with all male characters? Why don't girls enliven their play with siren wails, engine revs, and crashes? Even given the same "neutral" toys, you can look in on any group of three year olds in preschool and see that the boys are building long roads and the girls are making rooms and houses—if they play with blocks at all. The two sexes don't even play ball the same way. Yet who has said that boys must throw and girls must bounce?

Perhaps we have all said so, in subtle ways. For even the most scrupulous parents still find their efforts frustrated. The Jacobsons tried very hard to bring out Kenneth's gentleness. When Kenneth's mother gave him his first baby doll, he pulled it out of the box by one arm and then crammed it into a dump truck for a wild ride along the kitchen floor. No matter how she tried to interest Kenneth in cradling the doll or dressing it, Kenneth's fascination with dolls was confined to disjointing their limbs, cutting their hair, and opening their bodies to find their hidden mechanisms. Indeed, few nonsexist parents have been able to maintain a boy's interest in dolls much beyond the age of three, even when the same child cuddles a multitude of stuffed animals. And if their efforts do succeed, they may find themselves worried on another score: Does their son like dolls too much? However committed to equality we are, most of us sense that there is a boundary between the sexes we really don't want our children to cross, and liberationists have not said where that boundary is.

Children have been the great hope of the liberation movement. Their nature, as yet unspoiled by training, has been expected to prove, as Letty Cottin Pogrebin has put it, that

" '*femininity*' and '*masculinity*' do not exist. . . . They are fictions invented to coerce us into sex role behavior. . . . Someone female is feminine and someone male is masculine and all else is propaganda."[1] The sole difference between the sexes such feminists acknowledge is that required for reproduction—and that difference speaks for itself. We have only to know that a person has a penis to think of him as male and that a person has a vagina to think of her as female. All the other cues of posture, dress, attitude, or role on which we now depend in order to evaluate *how* male or *how* female a person is are unnecessary. In fact, feminists insist that these cues are learned at the expense of each individual's full potential for self-fulfillment and contribution to society. In the future feminists envision that we will not be taken aback by a man who weeps during a soap opera or keeps a weekly appointment with his hairdresser, for both sexes will one day be able to enjoy all sorts of pleasures without their choices casting doubt on their sexual authenticity.

The process by which nonsexism is supposed to come about within families combines good example, direct teaching, and censorship of materials that are considered sexist. Various books prescribe arduous review of all children's books, toys, clothing, and television shows that represent sexist views. For girls, "Little Red Riding Hood" is out, as is pink (one feminist mother went so far as to dye her daughter's whole layette a uniform black). By good example, feminists usually mean a rigorous sharing of parental roles so that a child can't get the impression that only men fix cars while only women wash toilets. Direct teaching is more straightforward, anything from pointing out that few women really worry about "ring around the collar" to vigorous campaigns against all-male Little Leagues or all-female cooking courses. Feminists also advocate open disapproval of a child's own sexist remarks or behavior. Their tenacious belief is that once we stop inculcating sex roles in our children, sex roles will disappear. Children will then be, in Marlo Thomas's words, "free to be, you and me," unconstrained by gender.

This idea is highly appealing. No longer would a boy who cried be made to feel like a sissy or a girl be forced to behave in pretty ways that were not truly hers. (Pogrebin, for one, would expunge the words "masculine" and "feminine" from our language.) These children would grow up able to contribute to society whatever their native talent and temperament could offer. A man could be male even if he found his gifts most apt for childrearing; a woman could be female and pursue mathematics.

The ring of justice is so loud here. Why aren't our children hearing? Of course, the nonsexist experiment is new, the children who are living it out still young. Neither their potential for nonsexist development nor their limitations are known, so that there are two ways to view their continuing conformity to traditional masculine and feminine stereotypes. Those who are committed to unlimited potential unhampered by restriction of gender blame society. They believe we have not gone far enough in our effort to "stop thinking of children as girls and boys." Those who believe there are limits blame nature. Girls will be girls. Boys will be boys.

This is a book for both groups. Whether we are for or against a change in our understanding of the sexes, change has already taken place. Feminism was not born yesterday. Women's lives have been extending outward from the home for more than two centuries, as is amply reflected in legal, political, social, educational, and economic trends. The movement is propelled by complex and enduring forces that are beyond the control of any particular ideology. To work or not to work is no longer a woman's choice; work is a necessity, not only in this country but also increasingly in all industrial societies. Little girls must be prepared for work outside the home. Little boys must be prepared for homemaking. It is more than likely that both will do both in the future.

So if our children are not easily meeting our nonsexist expectations, it is of concern to all of us. Perhaps they are telling us something important about themselves, or perhaps we are overlooking something important about ourselves. The purpose of this book is to explore our own and our children's total experience of being male and being female, so that, as we continue to adapt to the pressures of our time, we can consider how our children's growing up will best fit them for their future. We will want to know particularly if their brand of sexism is the same as ours, and if it proves to be different, what different function it might serve.

There is another purpose, too. Many of us who are responsible for raising children in this new nonsexist way are uncomfortable. Perhaps we can do it, but it doesn't feel right, and we don't know whether our actions or our feelings are at fault. An author committed to feminist principles writes, for example, of leaving her daughter with a neighbor so that she can pursue her career:

> As I write this, my three-year-old daughter is with another child and a babysitter at the home of a friend. Casey didn't want to go there—she has had four consecutive mornings and afternoons of babysitters and not enough mama. This morning she climbed into her bed, pulled up the quilt and announced: "I can stay here with you if I take a nap."
>
> Her crying and wanting me gets me in my gut—that part of me that was taught to believe that mama should always be there. So I spent extra time talking and snuggling and planning the playing we will do later. I am resolved about the kind of parenting I want to do, so I did take her to the babysitter and returned to work. But I am still torn by her pain and by my own conditioning.
>
> It is of paramount importance to me that I set a good example of what a woman is—someone committed to work and ideals in addition to child, husband, and home. But at the same time my training tells me that my child should come first, that my primary job as a mother is to serve my child while she is young. I and so many other feminist mothers I have talked with need to remind ourselves that the conditioning is wrong.[2]

We read this and waver. Although it is true that mothers have traditionally been the ones to dry tears, bake cookies, make appointments, go to school events, and buy birthday presents, these tasks can be shared with others; and women have a right—some would say an obligation—to work on a par with men. The mother shouldn't feel guilty—or should she? Who's wrong, the mother for feeling guilty or the daughter for feeling sad? Or are both their feelings insignificant compared to the social rightness of what is being done? If only mothers and children could be less connected to one another. But is that what we really want?

For we're also uncomfortable with the risks we may be taking if we are successful in our nonsexist childrearing. Daughters who aspire to be brides may worry us, but that worry pales beside successfully bringing up a daughter who doesn't want to marry and have children. Most of us are particularly frightened of what we might do to our sons. Even ardent feminists have their moments of acute uneasiness:

> When he lies on the floor at night, drawing or watching TV, quiet as he often is when he is alone, dressed in one of the long nightshirts he likes to wear around the house so that the elastic of his pajama pants won't hurt his stomach, I am acutely conscious of my desire to feminize him, to protect him from masculinity, to keep him from moving out of my world. Only rarely do I give in to this subversive urge—I have a fear of his losing his bearing altogether; that without masculinity in its most conventional sense, at least a part of it, he will falter, stay so close to me that he will not be able to walk away at all. Now he is passionate about dolls and cooking, delicate drawings, flowers and imaginary stories about winged swans who carry little boys to magical lands above the clouds and bring them home in time for dinner.[3]

This boy is five years old. When he was younger, he had often begged his mother to let him go outside wearing a dress. Is this the kind of liberated boy we want to bring up?

Not only are we toying with the traditional concepts of masculinity and femininity in an unnerving fashion—and then worrying about it; we are also tolerating unprecedented experimentation with the forms of family life and child care. Many children are now being raised in single-parent homes; more and more enter day care or other nonfamily arrangements in infancy. A small but growing number of children are being raised by mothers who chose to use the child's father for impregnation only. Some families have chosen to reverse male and female roles, so that the father rears the children while the mother supports the family. The number of children raised in homosexual families is growing, too.

All these experiments are related to the women's liberation movement, which has frequently criticized the traditional nuclear family as a sexist institution and hoped that it might be modified in ways more in keeping with nonsexist ideals. The participants in these experiments expect the result to be liberated children. But we do not yet know whether this will be the case or even whether nonsexist childrearing in any context will prove to be the path to liberated adulthood. We do not even know whether truly nonsexist childrearing is possible.

For these reasons—the need to adapt to change, the wish to become more comfortable with that adaptation, and the uncertainty of how best to achieve our goals—we ought to know a great deal about what actual differences between the sexes are and how they have come to be. Why are children sexist? Can we change their behavior, and if we can, is it possible that by doing so we may harm them? These are the questions this book will try to answer to the satisfaction of parents who are experiencing at first hand and day to day the difficulties of childrearing in a nonsexist context. Answers will not come easily. Emotionalism has supercharged this feminist issue. Arguments based on concepts of justice have been confused with arguments based on careful observations of children themselves. The nonsexist experiment is so young that there is less information to help us than we would like to have. This book will approach the questions methodically, pragmatically, calling upon observations made in several disciplines to reconstruct in some detail what happens as newborn babies begin, over the years, to exhibit sex differences we label "girlish" or "boyish."

One way to explore sex differences is to measure them. Sitting on the park bench, a group of mothers agrees that caring for their toddler sons is exhausting—they are forever having to chase them, they must always watch for trouble—whereas daughters of the same age require less parental energy and vigilance. We will see that psychologists are able to measure the mothers' informal impressions by, for example, attaching a gadget to a toddler's chubby ankle to see how much ground he or she actually covers and by closely monitoring a mother's every move to see how frequently she intervenes in her child's activities. Thus research can at least settle one aspect of the question of sex differences: either the park bench consensus is prejudice or the stereotype reflects a real difference between girls and boys.

Even when psychologists' measurements can show quite clearly that there is an actual difference between the sexes, they can't necessarily say why. If Susie really does break into sobs whenever her mother is cross at her, and her brother keeps right on messing in the cold cream, is that because the threshold for cying is biologically lower in girls than in boys or is it because Susie's brother has already learned that "boys don't cry"? This is one example of the nature/nurture controversy in which traditionalists claim sex differences are absolutely biological and feminists claim that they are entirely cultural.

A third "side," represented by many students of animal and human behavior, claims that this is not a valid question because it is based on the impossible premise that biological effects and cultural ones are separable. In this view, the proper question is: How are biology and culture related, and how does their relationship result in the behavior we observe? The example most commonly used to illustrate the point is human language. Human infants come "prewired" to learn language, provided their environment offers them one. Without the prewiring—in the case of a baby chimpanzee, say—human speech can't be learned (popular literature to the contrary, there is no such thing as a talking ape), even if the baby is raised in a garrulous family. Yet with all the wiring in place, babies who don't hear speech don't learn to talk. The issue that therefore has come to engross social scientists in fields as diverse as ethology and paleoanthropology is the origin of culture itself, for it may be that for any universal behavior—Janey playing house or Arthur kicking cans—the origin of the behavior and the origin of the culture that supports it turn out to be one and the same. If there is a common origin for an individual's nature and his culture's nurturing, then the either/or, nature/nurture question doesn't make sense. We must wonder under what conditions both originated and for what mutually supported advantages.

Human culture originated before written records or art, so its development must be pieced together indirectly. By looking at sex differences (and sexism) among our closest relatives, the chimpanzees, and also at the record of human culture as it has been reconstructed by paleoanthropologists from the remains of our ancestors, the hominids and early man, we can try to prize out the very roots of sexism.

The evidence gained from research into cultural origins suggests the novel view that babies are born equipped to become masculine or feminine in keeping with their biological sex provided their society responds to them in certain ways, and their society does respond to them in certain ways because culture itself is the result of evolutionary processes as deeply rooted in our biology as the contagious laughter of our babies—or their readiness to become girls and boys.

If that is so, we should be able to see a meshing of baby behavior and adult responses that guides the development of masculinity and feminity from the moment the newborn baby, conveniently born in the nude, announces his or her gender.

And, indeed, we can. After long years of tedious observations, researchers are beginning to make out the bare outlines of an intricate choreography performed by the baby and his or her family that over the years of childhood almost always results in the zany antics and the delicious charms we call boyishness and girlishness.

The dance, performed quite unawares by both partners, is a very long and very complicated one, and there sometimes can be mismatches between the way the baby behaves and the way adults around him or her respond. Purposeful mismatching is exactly what some feminists recommend: boys should be given baby dolls to cuddle, and girls should be given balls to throw no matter where their eyes wander, their hands stray, or their feet propel them in the toy store.

Is the result of mismatching a liberated child or an injured one? There are two ways to answer that question. The first is through clinical work with children who answer the description of the liberated child—the boy who loves Barbie dolls better than baseball, the girl who insists on football and no frills. The outcomes of such studies will worry most readers.

The second way to explore whether mismatching is a suitable method of rearing boys and girls is to consult the children themselves: What do they want for themselves, what do they wish to be like, how do they perceive masculinity and femininity as they grow up? Children's answers usually accord with what parents, to their delight or disappointment, have noticed.

Watching our children—Jenny, Ned, Sarah—as they go about their lives at various ages, we're struck by the amount of effort they put into being boys and girls. Certainly parents don't push their sons to play Superman at five o'clock in the morning or make popsicle sticks go bang for want of a better gun. Studies show, in fact, that parents expend considerable effort trying to tame boyish outbursts. Yet the effort is wasted. Boys toss stones, slam doors, and join private clubs, just as girls bake cookies and whisper secrets, even when their parents are unimpressed with these particular expressions of gender. These childhood behaviors are often as surprisingly rigid as children's opinions about who can and can't be president, so that if a little girl is determined to wear frilly clothes, we will get nothing but arguments if we insist on pants. This doesn't seem germane to today's world or even obviously related to gender roles as modern parents express them, yet it is just what we should expect if there is a built-in system for becoming masculine or feminine.

What is the relationship between that built-in system at work between parents and children and adult sex roles in society at large? This, finally, is what we must come to grips with because many of us now seem to be experiencing a painful incongruity between how we would like our children to turn out and how they insist on being. We will have to face the fact that the entire process by which a child comes to know himself or herself as a boy or girl, to express that gender socially, and to live it functionally is a tenacious program for the difference between males and females. The fact of masculinity and femininity cannot be changed. There are real differences; there are real limitations.

But by the time we have come that far in this book, we will understand both differences and limitations in a way that is far removed from the superficials of who is to make speeches and who is to mend socks. The differences as we will understand them here go back very far into our evolutionary history, have been crucial to our adaptation as a species, and continue to be central to our adaptation now. Our children's apparent failure to disregard the stereotypes of their sex, as we will look at it again toward the end of this book, is not the problem it appears to be.

For how children express their gender at three is quite different from how they express it at eight or at eighteen. Were a grown woman to express her gender by giggling, we would find it childish, not feminine. And if all boys who crash cars at the age of four were still doing that in adulthood, we would vote to abolish masculinity on the spot.

Luckily, sex roles develop and mature according to a time-table, much as do the stages of language development or the ability to draw a picture, and more mature forms are continually superimposed on earlier ones.

By looking particularly at children's own views about the sexes—when they are four, six, twelve, and older—we will see that even how children think about gender is determined by age and develops according to a rather strict timetable. The simple truth is that the children we are raising now are not yet old enough either to behave or to think in nonsexist ways. This should be a reassuring thought, because it means that hating girls or adoring Barbie dolls is, like falling in love, a passing event rather than a permanent condition. In the end, we will be happy to note that Sarah, who so wants to be a princess, may yet become a professor.

2

THE SENSE OF DIFFERENCE

A gang of little boys, ranging to the borders of the neighborhood, tussle with one another, aim rocks, hold impromptu contests, and plan elaborate strategies. For all the world they look as though they are practicing to fulfill the sexist stereotype. The neighborhood girls cluster close to home. Their hands are busy with little tasks—fussing at their dolls' hair, stringing beads—and their tongues are busy too. They seem in training for the motherhood and mending that feminists disparage.

Are we doing this to our children, or are these differences between boys and girls natural? Are women more nurturant by nature? Do girls cry more? Are males active and females passive? Or are all such contrasts fictions shaped by sexist storybooks and self-fulfilling playthings? Under pressure from feminists and out of their own sense of justice, psychologists have made a valiant effort to debunk sexist myths. From the results of more than a decade of intensive work, some have tried to create a new, feminist psychology that would wipe away cobwebs of assumption and reveal an egalitarian basis for human—not male, not female—development.

This is not an enviable task. Extreme persistence and hard work have barely created a dent in the mountainous volume of evidence to be sifted through. Supposed differences are many, as are supposed equalities, and few can be studied directly. Broad categories must be broken down into observable and measurable components. What are the components of passivity? If a child sits for hours over a puzzle, is that child passive because he is not being active? Perhaps he is mentally active and aggressively persistent. If a child is active in infancy, will that correlate with activity levels later in life? Does the activity yardstick used with a newborn—time spent awake, frequency of startle reactions, amount of random motion—have anything to do with the measurement registered three years later on an activity meter attached to the child as she plays in nursery school? Does the activity level have meaning unless we can also measure how organized and how effective the activity is? A burst of activity, after all, might be a tantrum, and those of us who have dealt with tantrums would have a hard time deciding whether they are active protest or helpless disorganization. And finally, is an active person really the opposite of what we mean by a passive person? We should not be surprised that psychologists, though armed with measurements of all sorts, have difficulty knowing what they have measured and what the measurements mean.

Nevertheless, some myths—sexist and nonsexist—have been laid to rest. Some true differences between the sexes have been found.

The most complete review of research into sex-related differences was published by Eleanor Emmons Maccoby and Carol Nagy Jacklin in 1974. They reviewed more than 1,400 studies in 86 categories that covered both sexes from birth to college age, with a few studies from later adulthood. Their book *The Psychology of Sex Differences* fills 627 pages and represents libraries full of original research reporting.[1] Most of today's feminist claims that the sexes are more similar than different originate in Maccoby and Jacklin's analyses, and rightly so. For Maccoby and Jacklin found most stereotyped sex differences to be more myth than reality. Such findings did not, however, recreate the sexes as identical.

Maccoby and Jacklin's procedure was to chart all reports that met certain scientific standards by category of sex difference under study—crying, competitiveness, coordination. They then entered the results on a chart: no sex difference found, or a sex difference found in favor of males or of females. They were very conservative. Only those charts which, when differences did appear, clearly favored one sex were considered to indicate a trend.

One unequivocal result, no matter what your school-age boy says, is that girls aren't "dumb." Males and females have equal IQs. This should not surprise anyone, because IQ tests are designed to be sex-blind. While such tests are being developed, any portion that biases overall results in favor of one sex or the other is deleted. Thus, males and females have equal IQs by definition. Maccoby and Jacklin's charts show that up to the age of ten, boys and girls also score equally on both the verbal and the math portions of IQ tests. After ten, girls begin to show superiority in verbal skills, and this superiority continues throughout adulthood. Girls surpass boys no matter how their verbal skills are measured. They excel at a mechanical level in spelling, punctuation, and vocabulary; in conceptual areas such as reading comprehension and understanding logical relations expressed in verbal terms; and in productive aspects of language such as verbal fluency and creative writing. By thirteen, boys begin to score significantly higher than girls in mathematics, and they too maintain their edge from then on. This is so even when the girls and boys being tested are selected for giftedness in mathematics, are highly motivated to do well in math, and have all taken the same math courses.

Attempts have been made to trace verbal and mathematical ability back through childhood to infancy, but the trail is faint. Fathers often tease a daughter that she hasn't stopped talking since the day she was born, but most tests during infancy and toddlerhood reveal no differences in verbal ability. When a difference is found, it is the girls who vocalize more and respond more to others' vocalizations. Language acquisition follows a similar schedule in both sexes; girls may have a natural edge, but Maccoby and Jacklin claim it is slight.

The difference in math scores after age thirteen seems to reflect an underlying male talent for spatial relations; the sexes remain the same in arithmetic ability. In many separate tests of people's ability to manipulate objects mentally in two or three dimensions, males definitely outperform females, but no early forerunners of this ability have been found. Preteen children perform the same, and no one has figured out a way to test spatial relations abilities with infants.

One possible source of difference would be a preference for one mode of perception over another in infancy. Baby daughters, many a parent reports, are spellbound by the sound of a voice and attentive to music. Is this the seed of later verbal ability? Parents also believe their baby boys are more fascinated by sights—venetian blinds or newspaper head-lines—and naturally gravitate toward the nearest toolbox. So far, results on both scores are inconclusive.

In spite of identical IQs, girls get higher grades in all subjects during elementary school. Could it be that girls excel at some particular type of learning that gives them this early advantage—and could the same style hamper them in later life, allowing boys to catch up?

Many learning processes have been studied, from rote learning to higher analytic processes. Researchers have identified only one intriguing phenomenon. After watching a movie, girls may recall more incidental information than boys do, without any loss of pertinent information. But there really does not seem to be any difference between how the sexes learn, just as there is no difference in overall IQ.

Are boys more creative? This is a particularly touchy question at dinner parties when someone holds forth on Bach,

Einstein, and Rembrandt. Certainly male chefs think they are more creative cooks than women, but then many women find men fools in the kitchen and confine them to the bar-beque. For testing purposes, creativity is defined as "produc-tion of associative content that is abundant and unique." When children are asked to produce verbally, girls are supe-rior in measures of creativity from the age of seven on. In other areas, there is no measurable difference.

Perhaps—according to a popular feminist view—men's ultimately greater success in the larger world is explained by low female self-esteem and motivation for achievement. However, sit in on any elementary school classroom and you're bound to notice that it is girls who represent our ideal of achievement motivation. Their neat papers adorn the walls. They raise their hands. They aim for all As and often get them. As Maccoby and Jacklin's analyses verify, girls respond well to external standards from teachers and parents and also formulate internal standards by which they measure their own achievement. Girls, as teachers have often guessed, are "good." Indeed, the boys are the ones who need an extra push in the form of competition from other boys. Since nei-ther sex views grades as competitive during the early school years, boys are less motivated to do well in school than girls are. Competition continues to be an important ingredient to males. When college men are measured on nonacademic tasks, persistence improves if other men are watching, as does the quality of performance. Girls and women are quite un-moved by an audience of either sex.

Girls have been thought to be somewhat less curious than boys, to explore novel situations less readily, and to take fewer risks. No difference has shown up at most ages, but between the ages of three and six boys do appear more curi-ous and willing to explore a novel situation. During this same period boys also tend to show a higher activity level than girls and to act more impulsively, at least in the laboratory. By middle childhood cross-cultural studies have shown that boys are found on the average ranging farther from home than girls. The reason usually given is that boys have herding, hunting, and farming chores to do whereas girls are made to babysit. In our own culture, however, where boys aren't shepherds and girls aren't nursemaids, boys still range farther and girls tend to stay closer to home.

The question of low self-esteem presents a paradox. In spite of the fact that both men and women (and girls and boys) devalue female occupations and also rate "ideal" masculine qualities higher than "ideal" feminine qualities, girls and women don't report low self-esteem. Females at all ages report that they are well satisfied with themselves and with their lives. Only one age category reveals vulnerability. In a study reported by Maccoby and Jacklin, college women reporting at eighteen and again as graduate students at twenty-six showed a drop in self-esteem during that period, and college women were the subjects of Matina Horner's well-known "fear of success" studies, too.

During the college years women lack confidence, too. They consistently predict low scores from themselves on various tasks, and when their scores come in, are likely to be dissatisfied with their performance even though they do better than they predicted and as well as men performing the same tasks. Good performance is often ascribed to "good luck," as anyone with teenage daughters may have noticed. Younger girls, however, have no trace of that "Oh, I just know I'm going to fail" attitude.

In contrast to girls and women, boys and men report higher self-esteem than seems warranted by the facts. They paint themselves in glowing terms. A ten-year-old boy, asked to estimate his relative position within a group, tends to place himself higher than his pals place him, even though the rate of agreement is very good among the boys for all positions other than their own.

A similar phenomenon differentiates males and females when fearfulness is studied. In actual fear-producing situations, boys and girls from two to six are frightened by the same things and with equal frequency. Above that age, self-rating scores are used, and here girls and women admit to higher anxiety levels about everything from snakes to exams.

At the same time, boys and men tested on lying and denial tend to dissemble about anxieties their examiners feel to be universal. For example, they may answer "No" to the question, "Do you sometimes dream about things you don't like to talk about?" Self-rating therefore doesn't show that females are more timid than males, as it doesn't show they have lower self-esteem; but the results may hint that males have somewhat different ways to keep themselves feeling good. Behind these rather remote testing procedures there is the little boy who arms himself with plastic pistols to face the first day of nursery school and the little girl who simply weeps and clings. Obviously, they're both scared stiff.

What about that crybaby girl? "Crybaby" is the great taunt of the boy gang to the "sissy" and, to be perfectly honest, many women will admit to ready tears in a bewildering variety of circumstances from soap opera weddings to relief at a lost child found safely in a neighbor's home to the finale of a nasty argument. Here the researchers are wildly disappointing on the whole, but do offer a few tantalizing details. The first disappointment is that reports on crying are limited to very young children.

At home, preschool boys cry *more* often than preschool girls. They cry when they object to restrictions or routines; they cry when what they are trying to do doesn't "work"; they cry when their mother leaves. But judging from the fact that these tears are shed among signs of frustration and anger—a boy may pummel the door through which his mother has just left or give it a kick for good measure—crying seems to be a way for these two- to four-year-old boys to voice their complaints. Girls tend to cry for help. At nursery school, girls more often cry because they are hurt, boys because they are frustrated with some recalcitrant object or adult demand. Although researchers don't speculate about whether a pleading quality as opposed to a protesting quality signifies another possible difference between boy and girl toddlers, we, as parents, can imagine a real difference in our response.

In the same situations that make them cry, boys show bursts of temper. So do girls until about eighteen months, when they begin to lose their tempers less frequently while boys remain at the same level.

Females are often thought to be more socially oriented than males, more concerned with how their peers respond to them and more sensitive to the moods and needs of others. Studies have not borne out such sweeping generalizations. During the preschool years, both boys and girls stick equally close to adults in general, although a girl may stick closer to her mother while a boy protests his mother's leaving more vigorously. Girls have been found to seek help from teachers more frequently.

By the time they are four years old, both boys and girls segregate themselves by sex while playing, so you can expect no-girls- or no-boys-allowed birthday parties to begin at this tender age. Preschool boys already show a particular pattern in their social relations with other boys. Mark cavalierly refers to "me and the boys" in nursery school, meaning the three or four boys with whom he always plays, sharing in a "monster" hunt or one of those doomed attempts to build a "real" car. These patterns are not seen among girls.

By seven, male groups have grown larger, while girls still tend to cluster in twos and threes. Friendships take on a different quality. Girls exchange secrets. They stand closer to a friend the better they like her. Boys are not affected in this way by degree of friendship. Whether a boy likes or dislikes his playmates appears to be irrelevant, for a group assembled for any given purpose is composed of those boys who have the needed skills. Charlie, no matter how obnoxious he is, may become one of the gang if he has good ideas for games or projects. This is not so with girls, who would exclude Cindy simply because "we don't like her," no matter what skills she has or how good her ideas are.

Contrary to popular opinion, tests show that girls are not more likely than boys to respond to peer pressure. Results hint in the opposite direction: boys may measure themselves more by what the other guys think of them than girls do.

Although girls throughout childhood remain more interested in books and television programs that have a social theme, as opposed to the adventure stories and science themes favored by boys, no differences in social skills can be found using the tools of research psychology. There is no laboratory evidence that girls are more sympathetic, more skillful at social "manipulation," or more frequently helpful. On the other hand, laboratory evidence is a crude measure. That both girls and boys reach for a kitten in preference to a gadget seems meager proof of equal nurturance unless we also get to see who cleans the litter box!

Sex differences are quite clear in a cluster of characteristics that are probably related: aggressiveness, activity, competitiveness, and dominating behaviors. For the purposes of reporting, Maccoby and Jacklin defined aggression to mean hostile actions such as hitting or threatening. Observations support the view that males are more likely to threaten a punch in the nose, and to carry out the threat, too. Study after study, whether under experimental conditions or observing children in natural settings both in our culture and others, shows boys to be more aggressive than girls. Nonsexists have countered that aggressiveness may take verbal forms as well as physical ones and that here girls will prove to be more aggressive than boys. They are half right. Girls tend to use verbal aggression more frequently than physical aggression to get rid of a pesky brother, putting him down rather than shoving him away. But they are behind boys in both departments. How aggressive are boys toward girls? Very few aggressive encounters occur between the sexes in childhood. When they do, they tend not to escalate into a fight or even into a prolonged display ("My dad's stronger than your dad" "He is not, my dad can lift a whole truck!") as they might between boys. Either a boy's aggressiveness is inhibited when he is faced with a girl, or the girl fails to react in a way that would encourage aggression. Whatever the reason, aggression is more commonly and more vehemently expressed between boys.

Feminists have claimed that males dominate females. According to the studies analyzed by Maccoby and Jacklin, males dominate other males; they do not dominate females. This is as true in childhood as it is in adult life, when investigators are similarly unable to find that one sex or the other dominates in relationships between them. Marriage studies, for example, have not turned up any dominance patterns. Both individuals in a couple apportion decisions between them so interdependently that neither husband or wife can say which of the pair is dominant.

This apportioning may begin early. In the only study that hints at male dominance over females, boy-girl pairs from five to nine were given a single sheet of paper and two crayons—one color for the boy, a different color for the girl. They were asked to draw a picture together. All but the kindergarten pairs seemed to show male dominance: the boy's color established the main outline of the drawing and his color covered more space. The girl's color filled in details and covered less space. But whether the girl feels dominated or the boy feels dominating is not known. More likely they apportion the job on some other basis, each according to his skill and pleasure.

Both sexes dominate, it seems, but to different ends. When a six- or eight-year-old girl is bossy, she is likely to dominate in the name of safety or of standards of conduct. "Come down right now," she will command a brother who is climbing a tree. "Mommy says it's time for dinner." A three-year-old girl may dominate a playmate by telling him he's the daddy, thrusting a briefcase into his hands, and ordering him to go to work. Boys assert themselves over other boys—"Go tell Bobby to come over here," "Find the ball we lost yesterday,"—to express their dominance. Big brothers keep a little brother in his place by assigning him to the outfield.

Both sexes agree as early as nursery school that boys are

"tougher" than girls. Groups of boys agree with one another when asked to rate each individual on a scale of toughness. Girls use that measure of dominance, too, but they often disagree when rating one another within a group, and the order itself changes from week to week.

If preference for one game over another reveals any degree of competitiveness, boys are more competitive than girls. Children will probably tell you that jacks is a girls' game, marbles is a boys' game. Both games are competitive, but there is a difference. In jacks, players compete to finish a certain set of motions. In marbles, players compete to take each other's marbles. Both games require skill and neither is athletic, yet in marbles winning or losing is "for real." And, as the children explain, boys play marbles; girls play jacks. Maccoby and Jacklin report the well-documented male preference for competitive team sports. They point out, however, that while an individual player may compete to beat the opposing team, he must at the same time cooperate with his own team. If game preference measures anything, preference for team sports may measure both willingness to compete and willingness to cooperate.

Complicated as the picture is, Maccoby and Jacklin conclude that males display more aggressive, dominating, and competitive behaviors than females. Could this be a result of some fundamental quality such as activity level?

A few studies suggest that newborn boys sleep somewhat less than newborn girls, but up to the age of one year neither is measurably more active than the other. After the first birthday, however, the picture changes. Although many tests still show no difference in activity, where there is a higher level of activity, it is the boys who are more active. Nursery teachers usually report higher activity levels for boys. There is, of course, a possibility that such observations are biased. In one test, the teacher reports of greater male activity were compared to measurements made by attaching activity meters to the same children. The meters showed no overall difference in gross movement. However, further analysis of this and of other studies using activity meters pointed to qualitative differences. An individual boy or girl shows the same activity level while playing alone, and for the girl that level stays the same when she joins a group of children. A boy's activity level shoots up when he joins a group of boys. We've all seen it: the boy lands on his pals' backs and they tumble playfully in a prelude to what will become the more sedate adult version of mutual male back slappings and hand shakings. When researchers studied test results anew, they also realized that the distance measured for each child's movements had not given a measure of that motion's vigor or forcefulness, or of how a group of movements are clustered in time—sudden bursts of exuberant bouncing, for example, as opposed to a steady rate of hopping on one foot. From all the results, Maccoby and Jacklin report a trend toward greater male energy output—which is exactly what those mothers on the park bench suspected or had learned from hard experience.

Just how well a child uses his or her body is a function of strength and speed coupled with coordination and visual perception. To hit a ball well, a child must hit fast and hard but also perceive the ball's trajectory and coordinate muscles to hit the ball at the right time and place. When such gross movements of large muscles are examined, boys tend to be superior in every measure. They are stronger, faster, more coordinated, and more accurate. When fine movement and small muscles are examined, girls tend to be superior to boys. They are more accurate, faster, and more nimble-fingered. In other words, a girl may look as awkward swinging a bat as a boy looks clumsy plying a needle. (This may be another reason why boys don't play jacks; perhaps they can't do it very well.)

Across cultures and at all ages beyond infancy, there seems little doubt that boys and men engage in more rough-and-tumble activity than girls and women. Does this reflect activity levels, competitiveness, aggression, or an ability to "take it"? A few tests, but by no means all, show female infants to be more sensitive to touch than male infants. By adulthood, other tests have shown that some women have a lower threshold of pain, and one study of pain tolerance has shown that men tolerate more pain than women. Results haven't been dramatic enough to say that boys in general are "rougher" than girls because they are less sensitive to touch and pain, but for a given individual, there is an intriguing relationship between touch sensitivity and pushy behavior. Children of either sex who have shown less sensitivity to touch as infants show greater persistence in attempting to get past a physical barrier between them and their mothers or between them and toys at the age of two and a half. Those who had greater sensitivity originally are less persistent in their efforts.

Most noticeable in all this behavior is the effect males have on other males. Boys react to the presence of other boys with bursts of activity, heightened aggressiveness, and dominating behaviors. These characteristics do not keep them apart, however; quite the opposite, boys form large groups within which they simultaneously compete and cooperate. Their performance and their persistence improve in competition with other boys or even in front of a male audience. There is some heightening and sharpening of response that boys experience in the company of other boys for which no female parallel has been found. Girls just do not act this way.

If we add to this already astonishing male constellation superior spatial relations and gross motor skills, it certainly looks as though a big chunk of the sexist stereotype is true. Boys really are boyish. And girls are girlish. Not only do girls lack well-defined boyish behaviors, but their chumminess and chattiness, the easy way they share their secrets and admit their fears, the careful way they do their work, and the closeness they keep to home and mother are stereotyped, too, in keeping with sexist notions. It looks as though the case is closed: there are measurable differences between the sexes and they are just what our grandparents would have predicted.

Still, to measure sex differences is not to explain why they are there. Although some sexist stereotypes—girls as cry-babies, boys as brave—prove to be chimeras, the differences Maccoby and Jacklin certify are ones feminists accuse society of foisting on innocent children. That position is hard to defend. If we do impose our children's stereotyped behaviors on them, they should be behaviors we particularly value or in which we see a special significance. Yet boys' rowdy greetings and girls' silly secrets are no more than amusing, sometimes annoying, and certainly irrelevant to most adults. Our sons care about Superman; we don't. Our daughters want to be princesses although they have never even seen one. Mothers don't teach their girls to play hopscotch. Fathers who are lawyers, professors, and executives don't share their sons' dreams of becoming firemen. Women do almost all the driving in suburbia, but it is their boys who are passionate about cars. Boys arrange their boyish hierarchies by rating one another on a toughness scale, although our adult hierarchies are based on far more subtle measures of leadership and talent. Little girls plant a goodbye kiss on the cheeks of mothers who wear hardhats or carry briefcases, and then settle down to play house with dolls. While mere toddlers, boys and girls begin to segregate themselves in communities where adult males and females don't practice sex segregation in any social activity.

Are the observed differences, then, *real?*

Readers who want an up-front answer to that question will be disappointed. By "real" differences, feminists usually mean ones that, because they are biological in origin, can be found at any age and within any culture. That expectation shows a misunderstanding of biology. Biological traits—even those we see as the most solid facts in an individual's life—can appear at any age. The fact that they don't appear at birth makes them no less "real." Graying hair is a biological trait, but two year olds don't have gray hair, even if they will when they are older. The emergence of both physical and psychological traits—graying hair as well as the capacity to fall in love—is determined by a timetable. Before the traits have emerged, however, there is no known way to detect their presence. A researcher looking at a newborn for evidence of a future capacity to do differential calculus is in as much trouble as one looking for evidence of graying hair.

Biological traits are coupled with the surrounding environment in very interesting ways. An example is that universal human trait, smiling, a behavior for which each baby carries a genetic program. The smiling program contains an instruction to respond in a certain way to a certain environmental condition and, in addition, an instruction as to how the environment is to respond. A baby is programmed to smile at an oval trimmed with a facelike arrangement of dots and bars; he is also programmed to "expect" that the oval will smile back. When some portion of this program fails—the baby is blind and can't see the oval he is to smile to, or the oval belongs to an acutely depressed mother who does not smile back—a fundamental human characteristic, sociability, hangs in the balance. Lack of the "right" biological cue to the environment or lack of the "right" response from the environment hampers social development equally.

The ramifications of so simple a thing as a baby's smile are even more exquisite than this. Although adults respond to a baby's smile as if it were friendly, the baby may not "mean" his smile in that sense. There is evidence that another thing the environment is "supposed" to do is interpret the baby's smile for him, so that smiling stands for friendly feelings, signifies attachment and, as the baby smiles selectively to those he loves, becomes functional in his social relationships. In peculiarly impersonal environments, infants of even a year or two years old smile indiscriminately at any adult without meaning any special attachment to that individual and without even reflecting an elevation of mood. For such babies, smiling has not worked; they have not developed a capacity for love.

Yet almost all babies do become loving. The program almost always works because the baby and his environment almost always do what they are supposed to do. What adult can fail to smile at a grinning baby? What culture doesn't signify warm feelings by a smile? Still the point to keep in mind is that sociability itself is not a biological trait; sociability is the probable outcome of a biological program (more complicated by far than the smiling portion of it alone) that contains instructions both for how to behave and what to expect. It is the interaction implicit in the program that makes the smile make sense. The social function of smiling is so sensible that, even without the sophisticated probings of researchers, we assume both the gesture itself and the meaning it carries is deeply rooted in our past, arising somewhere in the ancient ground of human evolution.

Judging from the intricacy of the smiling program and the grand design it serves, we can feel reasonably assured that can-kicking boys and doll-cuddling girls do not come about just through sex-linked genes for kicking or cuddling or just through sexist training in the proper treatment of cans and dolls. We are more likely looking at meshing components of a program, the usual outcome of which is recognizably masculine or feminine behavior.

We chafe at this interpretation because as adults we feel we run our culture. We are free to change customs and institutions and free to mold our behavior to the shape of our ideals. Regardless of what is written inside our newborn's fuzzy head, we can meet her expectations with surprising responses that will bring her around to our modern point of view. Before we wax so grand about ourselves, however, we should try a humbler approach. Our culture—all culture—may itself manifest our biological program, may itself be deeply rooted in our past. Sexism may not have been invented; it may have evolved.

3

TEN MILLION YEARS OF SEXISM

The origin of sexism is central to the nagging problem of how to raise liberated children. Must parents feel they can't control Johnny's way of squirming out of their arms or Linda's way of worming into their laps? If sexist culture is an invention, we are not bound to honor these babies' inclinations. We parents should really try, by refusing to see Johnny's adventuring as masculine and Linda's cuddling as feminine, to liberate them from such stereotyped interpretations. But if sexist distinctions arose in the course of our biological evolution, long before we had what could be called a culture, they will be etched too deep to wipe away. Sexism will, in that case, manifest itself in our culture and in every culture as unconsciously—and as far beyond our volition—as dreams.

Just knowing that will save us bickering about lavender party dresses; maybe the battle was lost before it started, and we could save the wear and tear of hopeless encounters. More important, uncovering the origins of sexism will shed light on the puzzle we still haven't pieced together. Park bench impressions and laboratory measurements concur: there are sex differences. But what is the point of them? Or are they, as feminists claim, beside the point?

If our peculiarly human forms of sexism were invented, we would be surprised to find them in a close relative of man. But if they evolved, we should not be surprised at all. Our closest living relative is the chimpanzee. And chimpanzees are sexist.

Female chimps stay close to home. Males spend their day far afield. Females cluster with one or two best friends, their daily routine of gathering staple foods interrupted only to nurse a baby, break up a squabble, or scold a straying toddler. They love to fish for termites by poking sticks into the mound and nibbling off the soft, plump insects that cling to it. Males range in gangs, and their day is punctuated by whoopings and hollerings to advertise a bonanza crop they have found, by tense and silent patrols along the community's border, by vicious confrontations with strangers, and by stirring pig hunts. Hunting is an all-male sport. Males have little patience with termite fishing.

Patrol behavior gives the flavor of chimpanzee sexism nicely. Males on patrol do not stop to look for food along the way. Although silence doesn't come easily to chimpanzees, they move without noise. As the patrol nears the area where community territories overlap, the chimps become extremely alert and visibly tense (they appear to suffer a human sign of nervousness—a touch of diarrhea, an urge to urinate frequently). If they spot a foreign chimp's naptime nest, they make aggressive gestures toward it as though it were the stranger himself, and destroy it with a show of violence. As they reach the border proper, the males stare attentively toward the neighboring territory, often standing up to see better. What exactly happens when they do spot strangers—and this ranges from a silent retreat to a savage attack and even to murder—depends on many circumstances. Usually the confrontation is a noisy challenge, a show of strength that includes standing erect to throw rocks and sticks, and a brief chase.

Females who have no baby to tend sometimes tag along when males are on border patrol. But they don't behave the same way as the males. They hang back; their place is in the rear, and their contribution is to make encouraging noises at the proper moment. They are the cheerleaders.

After a patrol is safely back from the border, the members often take part in an astonishing ritual. At a waterfall or beside a rushing stream, the males gather like members of the winning team to whoop loudly, to stand tall on two feet, to stomp the ground and shake their fists, break branches from the trees and thrash them against the ground. Females don't take part in waterfall rituals, nor do they ever display power or find relief in such show-off antics.

Team discipline and team spirit among male chimpanzees rests on another difference between the sexes: social organization. All the males who are born into a community remain within it, and all of them are permanently and strongly attached to one another through a dominance hierarchy. One is the boss, who may have achieved this highest rank through "toughness" (he can punch the other guys out), through affiliation (he has friends in high places), or through more subtle leadership abilities (he is a smart cookie). Like boys in a gang or men in a corporation, each male knows his place in the hierarchy, all of them agree on what the ranking order is, and the order itself changes only gradually over their lifetime together. Even the lowest-ranking male is dominant over all the females.

Females, like little girls, don't bother ranking one another. Their chummy attachments fail to hold them to the community. Restlessly on the prowl during estrus, a female is easily seduced by a stranger and doesn't mind going to live with "the enemy" in a neighboring territory. This does not mean that females are unaware of rank. They, like us, fall for the captain of the team. The top-ranking male is responsible for a high proportion of the pregnancies in the community not only because he jealously warns off lower-ranking contenders, but because females seek his attentions.

Chimpanzees are considered by many to be a paradigm of promiscuity, and it is true that a female in estrus will copulate with many males (the only prohibited mating appears to be between mother and son). It is also true that chimpanzees enjoy sex for reasons other than reproduction. A male may court a female of his choice while she is still in puberty and has not yet come into estrus. He will fondly groom and kiss her and share morsels of his food when she holds out her open palm to beg for it (food is seldom shared between males). A male and female may feel so strongly about one another as individuals that they form a temporary alliance known as a consort relationship. During consortship, the couple remain close to one another day and night, and they may copulate both before the female becomes fertile and after she has become pregnant. Finally, the couple may leave the group altogether and go off into the forest for a few days or even a month—on a honeymoon, so to speak.

We have no way of knowing yet whether a male chimpanzee recognizes which offspring he has fathered or whether he treats them and their mother preferentially. Males are at least tolerant of infants, seem to enjoy dandling them in their arms when the mother is otherwise occupied, and can be downright fatherly toward an orphaned youngster.

Sexism among the chimpanzees is a bread-and butter-issue, for it guarantees that by not competing for the same foods in the same places, both sexes will get enough to eat. But chimpanzees, while they are close relatives, are not our ancestors. We cannot have inherited our sexist behaviors from them.

Indeed, chimpanzees do not rely on most of the behaviors we have sketched here for their survival. Consortship is not critical to their reproductive strategy, as tool using and hunting are not crucial to their nutrition. Chimps could probably survive quite well without sharing food, or standing up, or throwing rocks. But each of these aspects of their behavior is clearly linked to gender. Either it is practiced exclusively by one sex, like hunting and rock throwing; or it is practiced preferentially by one sex, like termite fishing; or, like food sharing and consortship, it is practiced between the two sexes rather than among members of the same sex. Further, these behaviors are among those known to be central to the evolution of humans. Looking at the skills and habits that are merely helpful to our closest modern relatives, we are looking at ways that once became crucial to the survival of our actual ancestors. Is it a coincidence that such behaviors are specialized by gender?

Very recently, paleoanthropologists have begun to consider that the constellation of behaviors that made human evolution possible was fundamentally sexual. There are several startling peculiarities about humans that set off this thinking. First, we are the only animal on earth that ovulates in secret. Neither a man nor a woman consciously knows when the woman is fertile. Humans, alone among the animals, are sexually attractive to one another all the time.

Related to our sexual availability—and our heightened sexuality, for no animal copulates as frequently as we do—is another unusual characteristic: our eye-catching ornamentation. A woman's breasts, full even when there are no babies to be fed, her plump buttocks, that coy tuft of hair that points like an arrow to the genital opening, are a billboard of sexual attractiveness. A man's genitals, again haloed in a burst of hair that is without known physiological function, are more prominent by far than an ape's. More intriguing, extreme differences of skin texture, musculature, fat distribution, size and shape, voice and hair pattern between the two sexes also differ widely among individuals of the same sex. We are redolent of individuality. Each person is sexually attractive—uniquely so—though as a rule, each of us is attracted to only a limited number of people, and only a limited number of people are attracted to each of us.

These two peculiarities of humans, our continual sexual activity and our prominent individuality, are as unique as our remarkable intelligence and similarly cry out to be explained. The probable explanation arises from an apparently unrelated question: Why is man bipedal? Scientists used to think we walked around on two feet because we needed our hands to carry the tools our large brains had enabled us to invent. But if that were true, the fossil record should reveal human antecedents in the form of a large-brained ape who walked on all fours.

Fossils have revealed the opposite. The earliest known hominid, a not-yet-human creature called *Australopithecus afarensis* who lived at least 3.5 million years ago, walked with a gait indistinguishable from ours, left footprints that could have been our own, and manipulated objects with hands that were virtually human. His brain was the siz of a chimpanzee's.

This shocking discovery left begging the question of bipedal gait. For if early relatives of man had functioned without tools (or at least without anything more impressive than a broken stone) and with only an ape-sized brain, why in the world did they need to walk on two feet? Some scientists have suggested that the answer has to do with the fact that *Australopithecus afarensis* fossils are found in open country. Squeezed out of the tropical forests that began to shrink during the cooler, drier weather of the Miocene age 15 million years ago, one or more ancestral ape species might have been forced to take up life in the open savanna. Once in the open, there would have been sufficient environmental pressure to select for those individuals who could stand—and run—on their own two feet. Terrestrial apes would have had to stand up to see over tall clumps of grass. They would have had to run from predators, for here there were no trees to climb, or defend themselves by throwing missiles as occasionally happens with chimpanzees today.

Professor C. Owen Lovejoy of Kent State University, a specialist in animal locomotion, feels this argument is nonsense. No ape, shambling along a few steps at a time with still clumsy gait, would be stupid enough to venture out onto the savanna. And if he did, he wouldn't have survived. An effective stride must have developed in the forest long before it became a useful adaptation for life in the open. Further, the advantages of a two-footed gait are not obvious. Bipedal walking is neither more nor less efficient than walking on all fours. As for running, two-footedness is a sacrifice. The average person's speed and agility can't compare to a chimpanzee's. The further back bipedalism is found in hominid evolution—the more distant in time from the emergence of human intelligence and material culture—the more mysterious it becomes. If it developed neither to escape predators nor to defend against them and was not really very efficient for walking or running anyway, what was it for?

The probable answer is that bipedalism improved our reproductive rate. Our sexual ways have been so successful that we have populated the earth with our kind. How have we fed our many babies? By carrying home the groceries—in our own two hands.

Biologically speaking, the fundamental obligation of each individual is to pass his or her genes along to the next generation. Every creature, whether a mussel or a monkey, has developed a reproductive strategy which, given that creature's unique environment, ensures it the best chance to reproduce. A mussel, which cannot care for its offspring in any way, puts all its reproductive energy into overproduction of fertilized eggs that are simply released into the sea. Only a tiny percentage survive to become the next generation, but because the mussel invests in quantity, a low survival rate is workable. There are always plenty of mussels. The more advanced a species, the more it tends to rely on quality care— or, to put it another way, better survival rates for fewer offspring. A monkey invests most of its reproductive energy in mothering the relatively few offspring she has borne, thus assuring that a high percentage will survive. There are plenty of monkeys too.

Primates have carried the quality over quantity strategy just about to its limit. Their large brains and long childhoods equip them with the love and know-how to become admirable parents, but each child must be parented for many years before its mother can afford another birth, and so each mother must live a long time to assure enough infants raised to adulthood to replace at least herself and her mate in the next generation.

A mother chimpanzee typically cares for a child until it is five or six years old, and does not become pregnant again during all those years. A female is not sexually mature until she is ten years old. Given chimpanzee mortality rates, she must live to be at least twenty-one if she is to replace herself and her mate in the population. If she lives to her full life expectancy of forty, her maximum number of children raised to maturity is still unimpressive. In fact, her reproductive capacity is so dangerously low that chimpanzees—along with gorillas, orangutans, and gibbons—have been headed inexorably toward extinction since long before man edged all his living relatives toward the brink.

At some point, there is a minimum death rate over which a species has no control. Adults, who must also manage to feed and defend themselves, have exhausted what resources they have to expend on each offspring, yet not enough of the few who are born survive to maintain the population. Is there any way out of this dilemma?

An individual can improve the mathematics either by reducing the interval between pregnancies so that more infants are born or by finding ways to invest more intensely in child care so that more infants survive. Or it can do both.

One way would be to move into an area where the living is easy, a Garden of Eden where food is there for the plucking. Chimpanzees, however, have never left the Garden. There is no more abundant environment on earth than a tropical forest, and whatever adaptations an ape can make to decrease mortality through defense and vigilance chimpanzees have already achieved. Any change in the present odds is limited by the time it takes to gather food. Were a mother chimpanzee to have babies spaced more closely together or care for each baby more intensively, she would need more efficient provisioning. In other words, she would need help.

Owen Lovejoy theorizes that when our ape ancestors faced a similar predicament many millions of years ago, their solution was to engage the help of males. Basing his speculations on very early fossils and the habitats in which they have been found, Lovejoy has pieced together a plausible tale of evolution from Miocene ape to early hominids.

During that half dozen or so million years, the habitat changed from tropical rain forest much like that which the great apes inhabit today to cooler, drier woodland verging on open savanna. Instead of retreating as the jungle receded—the choice of chimp, gorilla, orangutan, and gibbon ancestors—our own ape ancestor stayed put. To do so, even at a one-baby-at-a-time birth rate, it would have had to develop less casual ways of obtaining food.

Recall the unrealized potentials of chimps: walking, carrying, advertising food finds, sharing food, honeymooning. The pressure was on to develop these potentials to survive as the Garden became less productive. Each depended on the other, so that any improvement in one talent affected all talents. Extend consortship by a few months and you have a bond that persists through pregnancy and birth. It is advantageous for the male to help provision his mate, since her baby is certain to carry his genes. And, since food sharing improves the mother's reproductive rate, it is advantageous for her to keep the actual time of ovulation secret from him by remaining sexually attractive at all times. But not to everyone; unique, even private signals—face, hair, figure, inviting glances—are more helpful than arousing smells available to every male in the neighborhood.

Males, of course, can only provision if they walk and carry. As they lose the ability to grasp with their feet, their babies, too, can't hang on to their mothers well. Females now have an even harder time gathering while carrying a baby, so that they really must stay home more. This becomes possible as males, each with mates of their own, compete less and cooperate more in gathering food for the group. No longer held in check by limited gathering ability, females raise two, three, four children at the same time.

Fossils bear out the lessening of sexual competition among males. Over the whole period, male canine teeth, once real fangs compared to females', shrank to nearly human proportions. They were no longer necessary for aggressive display. By 4 million years ago, fossils reveal hands, hips, knees, and feet almost identical to our own. Indeed, these fossils are considered hominids, not apes, and the temptation to grant them individuality is so strong that they have been named—Cindy, George, Twiggy, Lucy. It is even known, from footprints and from a group killed in a landslide or flash flood, that they lived in families.

We can speculate that by then sex must have taken on a special significance: a bond between couples, an assurance that their unique devotion, while perhaps not eternal, could at least endure until the children had grown up. We can also assume that women's liberation from food gathering chores was short-lived. As families grew—as hominids became Homo—men alone couldn't have fed all those hungry mouths. Aunts and sisters must have babysat at home so that as long as a mother wasn't nursing an infant, she, too, could have gathered food for the extended family community. Perhaps she carried a large leaf or a mat woven of grasses— harbinger of the basket. Perhaps her husband carried a spear. Society was distinctly sexist.

By 2 million years ago, hominids had become humans. As the brain rapidly expanded, as tools became critical to their food-getting strategies, as human culture emerged, what became of sexuality—and sexism? The answer is, not much.

The rapid and astonishing growth of the human brain during the approximately 2 million years of evolution from hominid to Homo only heightened the need for difference between the sexes. Women were tied down more; men had to help out more—and all because of changes that were happening to their babies.

Lucy gave birth to small-headed babies through a cor-respondingly small pelvic opening. By about 2 million years ago, the adult brain of the earliest *Homo* was, at the top of its range, nearly double the size of her brain, and the pelvic opening had enlarged to match. By somewhere between 100,000 and 400,000 years ago, *Homo sapiens* had emerged, and his brain was prodigious. The human pelvis, the female's in particular, had enlarged both front to back and side to side, giving women a more undulating walking gait than men and a less efficient running gait. Other adaptations occurred in tandem. Pelvic ligaments loosened during pregnancy in preparation for the passage of a big-headed baby, whose skull bones did not come together at their edges, thus allowing for a certain amount of compression during birth. Still brains continued to get bigger.

As brains grew even larger, it became urgent to get the baby born before its head became too large to get through the birth canal. Yet the pelvis had reached an engineering limit, for any more width would severely interfere with bipedalism. Without a radical solution, human birth would have become impossible. The solution was for babies to be born increasingly immature, indeed premature. Today, a newborn's head, large as it is in proportion with the rest of its body, will grow to twice that size by adolescence. Our infants' brains are also physiologically immature, smooth rather than convoluted, many brain cells not yet connected with one another, and most of their insulating sheathing incomplete.

These premature infants of ours are terribly dependent. They will not even toddle until they are a year old, months later than a chimpanzee. An orphaned six-year-old chimp is quite likely to survive on its own, though normally it would accompany its mother for several years more. Human socie-ties have traditionally recognized twelve years as a lower limit for survival without parenting.

As infant and juvenile dependency increased, parenting intensified. Human parenting is not only more fussy in its details than ape parenting, it lasts much longer and is sustained by the most powerful emotions. Mothers are often caught quite unaware by the intensity of their feelings for their newborn baby, the exclusivity of their involvement, and the sheer time mothering takes. If hominid females needed help, think what human females need.

The more a mother must care for babies, the more her mate must care for her. Infant dependency increases female dependency, or so we have believed. But that view is incomplete.

The entire group depends on these years of mother love. How else are our premature infants to grow up, to reproduce, to assure that their (our) genes survive into the future? There is almost a wrongheadedness in thinking that one sex could be dependent at the expense of the other or that one sex could be independent at the expense of the other. For if one depends and the other supports, that is possible only if the supporter also depends, and as a dependent also requires support. There may be complementarity, so that each sex both depends and supports in somewhat different ways, but the entire evolution of the human race points to mutual dependency—we could call it interdependency—to meet the challenge of raising intelligent infants successfully to maturity. Interdependence is the hallmark of human society, and for 99 percent of human history that interdependence has been expressed in ways we now call sexist. The differences we rail against are the differences we have carried within us for 10 million years. That's why they won't go away. For us, for chimps, for Miocene apes 10 million years ago, sexism has spelled survival.

This view challenges feminist assumptions both that sexism was invented and that society is doing things to people—especially children—that are not natural to them. When sex-linked behavioral characteristics can be traced back 10 million years and also found in budding form in our closest living relative, it becomes increasingly difficult to suggest a point at which females were deliberately dominated, deprived of their rights, or forced from public affairs. Were the bad guys apes? Hominids? Homos? None of them could have invented sexism, for it flowed from their unique adaptations and had long been inherent in their way of life. Could there, then, have come a time when people's inherent sexism was recognized by a society that then used it for the conscious purpose of exploiting women? That's possible, but for what reason? Surely not to do damage to women, on whom the survival of the whole society relies.

Much more likely—and some feminists agree—a sexist theory that exploited women did so for the purpose of ensuring that there would be even more babies and that those babies would be raised successfully. But it is not only the women, chained to squalling kids and hot stoves, who are exploited by purposeful sexism. Men also must stretch their resources to the limit to meet the needs of growing families. As long as both sexes agreed that big families brought an economic gain that would help all those children along in the world, it's doubtful that either the mother or the father would feel exploited. Today's sense of exploitation arose only with the failure of that reproductive strategy. Now, the most successful children are likely to be those from small families in which both parents earn money to give them the education and polish that will serve them best. Quality reproduction seems more crucial than quantity reproduction just now, and feminism supports that strategy well. Indeed, feminism may share with sexism a fundamental concern for the best possible send-off of our genes into the next generation. We shouldn't be surprised. Both arose within human culture, and any culture, our own or apes', is an expression of what we are like as a species.

Culture did not descend on our ancestors or on us from an external source. We made it up—we still do—to safeguard the ways of life that work best for us based on our own experience. Like any other animal, we are made of stuff, organized in specific ways, wired to perceive certain patterns through certain senses. None of our inventions, no matter how impressive or innovative, completely transcends our human nature. Quite the opposite; culture serves to refine and express more exquisitely the potential of our raw material.

The more consistently and the more emphatically human culture expresses sex differences, the more ancient those differences must be and the more rooted in our biological past. The more fundamental our tendency to form couples, the more we should expect to find that tendency made urgent by the phenomenon of falling in love, ritualized in marriage rites, sanctified by religious systems, protected by law, and promoted by our grandparents. The more we have depended on men to band together, to run, throw, take risks, plan strategies, and venture far from home, the more we should expect to find informal customs and formal institutions that train boys for that destiny.

Nor is it correct to assume that our own culture, by elaborating and even exaggerating behavioral differences, has over these millions of years superseded the original biological basis that gave rise to it. Evolution is very conservative. Without environmental pressure that literally kills off those who behave in traditional ways or prevents them from having babies, a species changes only by a process of drift or barely changes at all. Until now, human ways of life and human culture have not been inimical to the ancient behaviors on which they are based, and so they are still with us. Theories that justify exploitation must certainly be fought, but today's battle, however it might improve the ways in which sexism is expressed, will not eradicate it from our culture.

We adults manage our culture, but we do not run it. We can attend to the details—specify what constitutes marriage or agree on what clothing we recognize as masculine and feminine—but we aren't biologically free to rid ourselves of coupling or gender identity. These limitations come wrapped within each baby and can't be shucked by growing up.

In what raw form might we expect to find the fundamental, biologically determined, anciently rooted behavioral
differences between the sexes? First, there are areas where we
should not expect to find differences. We should be unable
to find a yardstick by which we can measure differences in
dependency, for dependency should prove to be a human
condition, not a sexual one. We should be similarly unable
to measure differences in nurturance, as our evolution relied
on paternal as well as maternal bonds. We may, however,
find that nurturance and dependency, while not differing in
degree, differ somewhat in form.

There are three areas in which we should expect to find
real distinctions between the sexes because they are tied to
the ancient ways the family was provisioned—meat provided
by far-ranging, tightly cooperating bands of male hunters,
gathered foods provided by females who paced their work to
fit the necessities of childrearing in smaller groups and at less
distance from their homes. The first is the individual's center
of activity; the second is the physical quality of that activity;
the third is the social relations with other members of a person's own sex. Specifically, males should tend to explore toward the outskirts of the backyard or the community while
females should tend to stay closer to home. Males should
show more interest in, and spend more time at, practicing
throwing, racing, tumbling, and leaping, as well as mock or
real fighting. Females should be more interested and involved in small repetitive movements and less interested in
fighting. Males should tend to gather in larger groups and to
order themselves hierarchically within those groups, whereas
females should form smaller groups that are more egalitarian
in spirit. Although no overall differences in intelligence or
temperament should be expected, any slight differences, such
as competitiveness or skill in spatial relations, that support
these sex-linked patterns should be more commonly observed
in one sex than the other. Finally, we should expect to find
the building blocks of the most fundamental potential of all:

a strong tendency in both sexes to respond differently to their own sex and to the opposite sex.

These are just the distinctions psychologists have measured and that describe your typical gang of ball-throwing, team-joining boys and your typical pair of arm-in-arm, doll-dressing girls.

The typical boy or girl we think we see when we observe children in a group, however, vanishes when we look at each child alone. When we come to know each boy and girl very well, we are struck with the uniqueness of each and find it difficult to reverse the process and bunch them back together again into a typical boy or girl. The same is true of the measurable traits we have discussed, for though the results of testing hundreds or thousands of children creates a striking profile for each sex, the profile says nothing about any given child and may in fact be a very poor fit. In either case, once we focus on the individual rather than the group, sex differences prove elusive.

How can we explain the fact that certain fundamental traits such as aggressiveness appear to be linked to one sex or the other, but that there is also such a great difference from one individual to another, regardless of sex, that we cannot predict whether any particular baby girl will be more or less aggressive than any particular baby boy? Lovejoy's speculative reconstruction of human evolution points to the kinds of differences researchers have found. A rigid distribution of traits by sex, however, could not have survived environmental pressures during those millions of years of evolution. No culture could survive if its women could only pick blueberries or its men could only stick pigs. When men were skimmed from our own society to serve in World War II, women replaced them in every sort of job. Emergency shifts, or slow and gradual changes under less pressing circumstances, must have been taking place all through human history. Looking at our past, the difference between the sexes makes sense only if it constitutes an average—a statistical—difference with sufficient overlap and sufficient flexibility so that under the stress of environmental challenge, either sex can shift in either direction.

The very fact of such extreme variability and flexibility poses a problem for each society and for the children growing up in it. Every culture's basic unit is the family. However that unit is defined, whether marriage is monogamous or polygamous, families nuclear or extended, whether children are raised with their parents or in communal groups, the family is built on the bond of sexual attraction between male and female. No culture has yet felt it could afford, by blurring all distinctions between the sexes, to dissolve that glue. Men and women may be similar in temperament, dress pretty much alike, even perform very much the same functions; but gender identity itself must not suffer lest heterosexuality suffer too. Underlying the bread-and-butter issue from which our brand of sexism probably arose 10 million or more years ago is the most fundamental point of all: reproduction. If each individual child has some potential for both masculine and feminine behavior, if that potential can be socially manipulated, and if a culture chooses to adapt—as some are suggesting we do now—by emphasizing "unisex," how can a child learn to evoke and respond to sexuality in the opposite sex? What would make the child bother to become his or her gender at all? The fact of being male or female when not interpreted to mean masculine or feminine might remain as meaningless as an infant's automatic smile when no one smiles back.

Regardless of parental ideology, trying to achieve and consolidate a sense of being one sex or the other has evolved along with us (because otherwise we would not be here to ponder on it) and is built into the pattern of child development. The child does not care whether he or she is born into a culture that defines femininity by ribbons or body scars, masculinity by crew cuts or pigtails, as long as it is clear which way to go. Apparently, we have a hard time being unclear. How many mothers can stop themselves from sitting with a leg tucked under—the female way in our culture; how many

men can force themselves to sit that way instead of sprawled—
the male way in our culture? Almost all our little boys soon
sit sprawled and almost all our little girls soon sit tucked.
That sense of gender is not thrust upon the child by society.
It comes from within the child, although it is simultaneously
supported from without, just as the push to stand and walk
arises internally, although we still extend a helping hand.

Without some internal clues, the helping hand would
not be strong enough. To learn their native tongue, children
rely on built-in patterns as well as on specific models and
assistance echoed from outside. Those learning patterns fade
after a certain age, and it is never again as easy to learn a
language. Perhaps, in similar fashion, when children seek
their gender, they use those remnants of sex-linked behavioral patterns that evolved so long ago and that now appear
to us so obsolete; perhaps those templates also fade with age.
Without the helping hand, the slim clues that cause boys to
gang and girls to cluster are certainly not enough either. No
one thing is. Biological bases can be overridden, statistical
averages are only that, parents themselves have less influence
than they think. Yet some combination of all three must be
hard at work, for children vehemently, tenaciously, often in
opposition to adult notions and in ways unique to childhood,
seek out and loudly express their gender. What makes the
"neutral" infant become a boy or girl?

Perhaps as we explore the answer to this question, we
will salve another disturbing feeling: that for all the work that
has gone into studying sex differences, the results are not satisfying. What we can measure and put on paper fails to cap-
ture the sense of difference we feel, the intuition that
masculinity and femininity contrast with one another in profound ways for which there is no yardstick and which no
cluster of traits defines—but that are the differences that make
the greatest sense of all.

4

BABY POWER

Two new mothers are nursing their babies and comparing notes from their hospital beds. The first mother points out how snugly her day-old daughter curls against her body. The other draws attention to how her son rummages for her breast and laughs about his greediness. These mothers surely haven't had time enough to get to know their offspring, but on the basis of their babies' gender, they're already making observations about their babies' temperaments.

Until recently such easily made observations were all we had to understand how gender identity develops. Either traditionalists were right, and Alice really was born cuddly and feminine, while Alexander was born pushy and masculine, or more recent opinions were right and it was merely the mothers' expectations that led them selectively to notice and appreciate characteristics that conformed to masculine and feminine stereotypes. Meanwhile, almost no one asked a central question: What is the baby up to?

Recently, several paths of inquiry have focused on the question of the baby and what he himself brings to his earliest social encounters. From this work we will see that the two tiny babies nursing on their first day of life have a lot to say about how their mothers behave. Realizing how socially adept babies are will give us a new perspective from which to view the possible effects of even very slight sex differences in infancy.

Until a decade ago, layman and expert alike conceived of newborn infants as entirely dependent, passive, inexpressive, unresponsive to sights and sounds (or even incapable of perceiving them), and so blank in the brain that almost any mold could be imposed upon them. Since then, research psychologists have discovered—to their own astonishment no less than everybody else's—that human infants are born equipped to enter social life actively and even direct their own development. Researchers have discovered baby power.

Take, for example, the newborn baby. For nine months she has lived in cushiony warmth where sounds were muffled and only occasional soft light penetrated her mother's abdominal wall into the womb. The fetus has not had to participate in either her feeding or her breathing. But during the space of a few hours, this shielded, nurtured, inexperienced little life is mightily squeezed, then expelled so forcefully her nose may be flattened against her face and her skull deformed. Cold air plunges into her lungs, her own sharp cry assails her ears, she squints her eyes against the piercing light. No doubt, exhausted by the trauma of birth, she will soon fall fast asleep.

But no. Calmly, the newborn baby looks about, head turning, eyes scanning this interesting place. She is not likely to fall asleep for hours. In fact, newborn babies are awake for longer during the first day of life than they will be again at any time during the following month. (This special alertness of newborn babies is, however, masked by the effects of anesthesia and so was noticed only after natural childbirth became widespread in our culture.) Many stay awake, and stay alert, for a full six hours immediately after birth. Similarly, mothers, though they too should feel exhausted, report excitement and a reluctance to sleep away these memorable hours.

Perhaps it should not surprise us that when the alert infant and alert mother get together, they are very interested in one another. Take a look at a brand-new mother. Seeing her baby's open eyes and intent gaze, the mother swoops her face into view, stopping about eight inches from the baby's face. Their eyes lock. The mother smiles, raises her eyebrows, flashes her white teeth. Her face bobs and weaves as she coos and talks, lifting her voice high and lilting up and down in exaggerated sing-song. The mother moves to one side, talking baby talk, and the infant turns toward the sound. Again, their eyes lock. When her little daughter fusses, the mother picks her up and cradles her against her left side— whether she is right-or left-handed—where the baby hears the same heartbeat she has become familiar with during her months of fetal life. The baby snuggles her body close to her mother's. After a few minutes the baby stirs again. The mother lifts her to her shoulder. The baby turns her head to the side, and the mother tilts her head too, automatically supporting her daughter's head against her cheek. Upright now, the baby's alertness increases, and she starts studying her new surroundings again.

Enter the researcher, who whisks Alice off for some routine testing. What does he find? That the newborn baby is more attentive to a sight (her heartbeat decelerates, her body stills, she gazes intently) if that sight has strongly contrasting dark and light areas and is moderately complicated—more complex than a circle, simpler than a printed page. The sight will be even more interesting if it moves, nodding or swaying on the verge of the baby's focal distance, which, miraculously, turns out to be eight inches. The sight will prove most gripping of all if it is a human face. Alice responds to sounds, too, and turns toward the ringing of a bell. When given a choice, however, the newborn baby prefers sounds within a particular frequency range, the range of a woman's voice. And as with sights, sounds are favored if they "move," if they are not only high but also inflected.

All this the baby's mother seems to have known without any help from psychologists. She presented her face for her baby's inspection at just the right distance, where her child could see it most clearly. She riveted her baby's attention with her nodding movements and by increasing the natural contrasts of her face—widening her eyes to enhance dark pupils in their white background, parting her lips to reveal bright teeth. She has even made herself sound delightful by slowing the pace of her speech, lifting her voice, and slipping into the exaggerated inflections of sing-song baby talk.

Curiously, what the mother "knows" is what the baby "expects"—or at least is most prepared to watch and listen to. Most curiously of all, the mother goes into her extraordinary act right on cue, when her baby's alert expression and open eyes elicit her performance. Clearly, mother and baby are made for one another; their built-in programs have seen to that.

The mother seems to share with her baby a communication system of which she is almost entirely unaware. Although she has no idea that the upright position helps her infant stay alert, she hoists her to her shoulder just as her interest in the world begins to fade. The unconscious communication system seems to serve not only to regulate such states as alertness or sleepiness, but to maintain a vivid social life. We can get an idea of the social life between mother and baby by looking in on Alice when, sick of tests and hungry, she is returned to her mother for another feeding.

For an experienced mother, nursing is a simple business. The mother holds the baby's cheek to her breast, the infant turns toward the touch, roots for the nipple with open mouth, grabs hold, clamps down, and begins to suck in bursts interspersed with pauses. Each time the baby pauses, the mother jiggles him. When asked why she jiggles, both first-time and experienced mothers give the same answer: To wake the baby up, get him going again, speed up the feeding. They are quite wrong. Babies resume sucking sooner and finish the meal faster if they are not jiggled. The explanation for this apparently irrational jiggling lies in what happens during the pauses. As the mother jiggles, she lowers her head, often catching her baby's glance, and talks to him. He gazes back, his arms and legs go limp, and his face relaxes too (older infants let loose the nipple to grin and coo). The baby's pattern of sucking in bursts, then pausing, seems designed for a happy hour, not a meal-on-the-run. The baby initiates pauses for a little social break.

Meanwhile the baby is getting to know his mother. Breast-fed babies know their mothers by the smell of their milk after a mere two weeks; they turn to her nursing pad in preference to someone else's. At only ten days old, babies show that they have become accustomed to the care of a particular person, usually their mothers. If that person is replaced by another person, the baby is distressed and fusses during meals, crying more no matter how experienced and responsive the substitute may be. The baby does not know a particular person in the same sense as the two year old knows Mommy or Daddy. More likely he comes into the world prepared to mesh with the style of a particular person and gets to know her as a whole "package" of experience. Distress occurs when whatever meshing he has achieved—even within his first ten days on the job—suddenly fails to work.

This meshing concerns us because it is the first ground on which a mother's expectations, including gender-related ones, meet her baby, complete with his or her actual gender, head on, to negotiate a particular relationship between them. Each mother brings her own style to these social get-togethers. There are mothers who talk to their babies, chatting all day. Other mothers are quiet, but touch their babies frequently. Some differences in behavior can be explained by the sex of the baby. Maccoby and Jacklin report that mothers touch and hold their newborn sons more than their newborn daughters but talk to and smile more at newborn daughters than newborn sons.

Each baby has an individual style, too, and also a tendency to behave according to gender. Girls, more physiologically mature at birth, tend to be more organized than male infants. Their movements may be smoother, they remain alert for longer periods and also sleep a little longer. Girl babies vocalize more than boy babies but cry less. Many are more responsive to sounds than are boys and more sensitive to touch. Charmingly, newborn girls frequently smile—a reflexive expression once thought a mere grimace caused by gas pains but now known to be the fleeting precursor of the true social smile. Newborn boys show fewer reflexive smiles. Yet, there are also personality differences. Talk to a mother who has had several children and she'll tell you that her first was easily soothed by stroking or patting, and her second by lullabies; with her third, nothing worked—or what worked one weekend didn't work on Monday.

By spending hundreds of hours watching mothers and babies at mealtime, researchers have confirmed mothers' impressions of varying temperaments in their newborn infants. During a feeding, dozens of events occur. The baby sucks, winces, squirms, jerks, relaxes, lets go of the nipple, burps, falls asleep, hiccups, smiles, roots, cries, opens his eyes, tenses his face or softens his expression. His mother rocks, sits still, hums, is silent, adjusts her position, tenses, relaxes, gazes, smiles, talks, pats, strokes, lifts her baby, puts him down. Each event is a remark:

> *Baby, squirming:* "I'm uncomfortable"
> *Mother, cooing:* "Does this help?"
> *Baby, still squirming:* "No."
> *Mother, rocking:* "Is this better?"
> *Baby, relaxing:* "Yes."

Through such dialogues a mother and baby negotiate a feeding, each trying to accommodate to the other's style. When the mother and baby are well matched, the negotiation goes so smoothly the adult will barely notice it and the effect will be one of effortlessness. When the mother and baby are mismatched—and that is just as possible—the dialogue may be extended and frustrating. Often the mother's side, exploding in frustration, is actually spoken: "You don't want to burp, you don't want to eat, you don't want to be cuddled! I wish you'd tell me what you *do* want!" But even when the relationship is troublesome, a compromise is eventually reached in which everyone feels relatively comfortable. A mother to whom cuddling comes naturally learns to hold a "stiff" baby less tightly, less often, and at a greater distance than she would a cuddly baby, while the baby also adjusts to the terms they have worked out between them.

Why has this intricate communication by which mother and baby arrive at a comfortable meshing of styles escaped notice for so long? There are two reasons. First, it is technically difficult to record interactions in enough detail to see what is really happening. Second, we simply didn't know the system existed because it is almost entirely unconscious. Of course, we can see the cruder aspects. There's the mother who solves a feeding difficulty with her unyielding baby by letting him take his bottle on her lap instead of pressed into her arms; but by and large mothers perform most of the duet unaware of the cues, steps, rhythms, or phases of the dance.

Those who believe we can alter sterotyped responses to a baby's gender have not only failed to take into account the power a baby has to direct his own social life; they have failed to grasp that what is done unconsciously is not accessible to adult control. Alice's mother may have consciously insisted on blue jeans instead of skirts from the word go, but when her daughter, like most girls, insists on a softened response, she will soften. All of us do. What if Alice were boisterous? The likelihood is that her mother, unconsciously and in spite of her best intentions, would still soften her responses somewhat. We've all had the experience of mistaking the sex of an infant or toddler. As the parent corrects the mistake, we can almost feel our minds rearranging themselves to think boy instead of girl. Though what exactly is being rearranged remains unknown, the child's very face seems to change before our eyes.

If something in our natures primes us to behave more softly with a girl, we will unknowingly moderate our response even to a boisterous baby girl. Since compromise is the usual upshot, a baby who does not meet our expectations will have to move somewhat toward them anyhow, and also a parent will have to move somewhat toward the baby's expectations. Whatever masculinity or femininity we may find results from the mix of our wishes and our baby's commands, the recipe is concocted by the parent and the baby, not by the parent alone.

The unconscious patterns by which babies and their parents interact are so regular that they can be likened to the rules of a game. The psychologist Edward Tronick and his colleagues at Boston Children's Hospital uncovered the underlying rules of face-to-face play by videotaping adults and infants during hundreds of social encounters. Each baby, well fed, well rested, and feeling quietly alert, was seated in an infant seat. Mother, father, or one of the researchers was invited to play with the baby. The videotaped play interval could then by played back to see exactly what had happened between adult and child.

On the surface, what happened was unremarkable. We have all played these games of smiling, cooing, nodding, and patting with our own and our friends' babies and know we have special ways reserved only for infants. We repeat, "Oh yes, oh yes, that's my boy, that's my baby, oh yes." As the baby responds to us with a show of delight, legs churning, gurgling, we are sure to do an even stranger thing—we open our eyes ridiculously wide and form our mouths into an "O" shape as we lean close and coo. There is no other circumstance in which we spontaneously make an "O" face.

After a great deal of tedious analysis and replay, Tronick's group was able to discern the rules of the mother-baby game. For instance, there is a formal opening to the game, distinct phases and pauses, and the mother's "O" face typically appears only as the playing reaches a peak. A mother hardly ever makes this exaggerated face as her baby glances away, nor does her baby smile broadly while his mother turns her gaze. But are the rules of the game set by the mother, who is simply adept at fitting in with and anticipating what her baby is doing, or does the baby understand the rules, too?

To answer the question, mothers were asked to sit face to face with their babies as they had before, but they were not to move or speak for three minutes. Results were unequivocal and upsetting. The babies, animated and charming in previous play sessions, tried again and again to initiate play by smiling broadly at their mothers. When met with blankness, they would quickly turn away. By the end of three minutes the babies often lay slumped in their infant seats, soberfaced, chin buried in chest, sucking on a finger or rocking. There was no doubt that, in the baby's view, something had gone sadly wrong—and babies as little as two weeks old showed they were puzzled when the rules are violated.

Tronick also asked fathers to play with babies under the original conditions: the baby seated comfortably in his infant seat, the cameras recording an unrestricted performance. Not too surprisingly, fathers play the game differently from mothers, although the rules are the same. Mothers often contain their babies' movements by holding their legs or hips, and calm them with soft voice, slow speech, and repeated rhythmic phrases. In this way, mothers are often able to keep up quiet "conversations" with their babies for many minutes. Fathers more often poke their babies, pedal their legs, punctuate the game with abrupt noises, and altogether stimulate their babies to higher—but briefer—pitches of excitement from which the babies recuperate with rather longer periods of disengagement. The faster tempo and less predictable, excited quality of the fathers' game is evident by the time the baby is eight weeks old and may be noticeable even at four weeks. Although babies are equally attentive to both parents, there is little doubt that the social life a baby enjoys with his mother is distinguished remarkably early from the social life he enjoys with his father.

Yet parents don't "see" the part their baby plays, don't know to what baby actions they themselves are responding, aren't aware of even their typical "O" face or of the game plan they follow. The parents in Tronick's study were amazed when they saw their play replayed. The mothers who participated in the stressful still-face experiment reacted most dramatically. As Tronick reports, "Mothers often commented that the excited glee of their babies the next time they entered the alcove (often less than ten seconds after their still-faced exit) was the strongest indication they had ever had that their babies cared about what they did." [1]

Once we appreciate the contribution babies make to their own social life, and how much they care, we have to wonder anew about subtle sex differences in the newborn baby, for sex differences such as rates of smiling or response to soothing need not be consciously "seen" to influence interactions between parent and infant. Howard Moss, a psychologist at the National Institutes of Mental Health, studied thirty pairs of first-time mothers and their babies during eight-hour periods when the babies were three weeks old and again when they were three months old to see how such different baby traits influenced mothers' behavior. At three weeks, baby sons fussed more, cried more, and were more difficult to calm, while baby daughters were more often alert, more responsive to efforts to calm them, and slept an average of one hour longer every twenty-four hours. Mothers held their sons more at this age, moved and stimulated them more, and altogether spent more time attending to them. Girls, more mature and apparently less in need of physically supportive behavior to become calm or to remain alert, received less holding, moving, and stimulation—in fact, less attention altogether.

These mothers, Moss inferred, were not reacting directly to their infant's sex; rather, they were responding to their baby's irritability. At three weeks of age, Moss could predict how much handling a baby of either sex would receive from his or her mother by measuring the amount of time during which the baby fussed and cried. By three months of age, however, Moss's prediction no longer worked. Not that irritability had changed—boys were still more frequently dissatisfied and slept less than girls. But the more her three-month-old son cried, the *less* his mother now attended to him. Attendance on daughters remained unchanged, so the net effect was that mothers held their daughters more than their sons by a few months of age.

Moss could only guess why this might be so. Perhaps, he thought, attending to a baby girl was encouraged because it worked: when a baby daughter was picked up and cuddled, she rewarded her mother by promptly quieting down. A hard-to-please boy might not be so gratifying. If he remained fussy whether or not his mother picked him up, held, rocked, patted, or stroked him, she might not feel that her attention was worth the effort. In such a way small differences could modify the interaction between mother and child over time, shaping a pattern between them that does depend, however indirectly, on the baby's sex.

There are researchers who feel their measurements have captured some intriguing differences that become apparent around the end of a baby's first year. Psychologists Susan Goldberg, now at the Hospital for Sick Children in Toronto, and Michael Lewis, of Rutgers University, have made very detailed studies of infants in both home and laboratory settings and report several differences in a sample of sixty-four babies observed at six months and again at thirteen months. The most interesting observations are made at the later age as each child, accompanied by his or her mother, played for fifteen minutes in an ordinary small playroom equipped with nine everyday toys; the researchers also counted doorknobs, light switches, and so on as "playthings" for the purpose of observation. There was a chair in one corner where the mother could sit, but she was allowed to respond to her child in any way she wished during the session.

Only two "interventions" were asked of her. As the session began, the mother was to take the child from her lap and place him or her on the floor. At the end of the fifteen minutes, a barrier, similar to the side of a net playpen, was placed across one end of the room. The mother was then to place her child beyond the barrier, while she—and the toys—

remained on the other side. Observations were made every five seconds during the session and included not only what the child was doing but also how he or she was doing it and where. For example, the observer noted that one child played with the lawnmower push toy by wheeling it over the stuffed dog, squealing with delight as he glanced at his mother from a position on the squared-off floor that was six feet from her side.

Boys and girls behaved differently after both interventions and during the entire experiment. The most popular toy with both sexes was the push toy, closely followed by a set of blocks; the observers rather stiffly concluded that "the toys which received the most attention were those that offered the most varied possibilities for manipulation." How they were manipulated is another story, for the boys might be more accurately described as wielding the toys—they banged the push toy against the floor, mowed it over other toys, and swung it through the air. We could wish that the observers had recorded the sound effects too: how many crashes of blocks? How many squeals and vrooms? But even in their dry reporting a certain flavor comes through as the psychologists remark how the boys spent "somewhat more time" in vigorous motion and in twisting the doorknob, reaching for the light switch, and going for the tape that covered the electrical outlets.

Girls were altogether more sedate. Instead of mowing through blocks and making their mothers wince as they swung push toys about, they tended to accumulate several toys all in one place, seat themselves among them, and play quietly using small rather than large muscle movements.

When, at the end of the session, the barrier separated the child from his or her mother and the toys, the two sexes used entirely different strategies to get out of their predicament. Girls were likely to stand smack in the middle of the barrier (where all the children were placed), crying and motioning for rescue. Boys tended to move to one end of the barrier and—though the effort proved fruitless—try to batter, wrench, or squeeze their way past it.

From the very beginning of the experiment, when each child was placed on the floor, girls were more reluctant to leave their mother than were boys and usually wasted no time getting back to her. Throughout the fifteen minutes, girls spent more time near their mother, came back to her more frequently, and maintained contact more continuously through touching, glancing, and vocalizing. Boys were more likely to go farther from their mother, perhaps even to the farthest corner of the room, to spend less time close to her, and to check in with her less frequently.

The researchers were not surprised that girls were "closer" to their mothers than were boys, for when these same children were observed at home at six months, mothers touched, talked to, and looked at their daughters more than their sons, just as Moss noted in his study of mothers and infants. It seems obvious that a child who is touched more at six months will keep in touch more at a year. That supposition turned out to be quite exact for boys. The more a mother had touched her son at six months, the more he sought out physical contact with his mother at thirteen months. The relationship between being touched and touching was not so straightforward with girls.

True, those girls who had received more touching from their mother now touched their mother more frequently. But so did those girls who had been touched the least. Indeed, even daughters whose mothers struck the researchers as "rejecting" at six months continually sought contact. That was not the case with boys whose mothers were similarly rated.

Research psychologists who confine their observations to brief periods in laboratory settings are understandably more comfortable with reporting than with explaining. What they gain in precision they lose in perspective. Those hugging or nonhugging mothers, those clinging or nonclinging children had been sharing nearly every minute of their waking lives for more than a year; it's no wonder that two glimpses haven't really much to say about why Joanna is sitting in square one while Jamie is swinging a push toy in square nine. What happens between the first and the final months: to the game, to negotiations, to the relationship between a baby and his or her parents?

By following the game as it is transformed by the baby over the course of his first year, we can get a rough idea of what is going on. By the time a baby is four months old, the original game of early infancy begins to falter. The baby looks away from his parent down toward the strap that holds him in his infant seat and begins to finger it or bring it to his mouth. He looks up, but his eyes only brush across his parent's face, settling instead on his father's watch or his mother's pendant—should she be brave enough to wear one. These are clearly what he thinks they should be playing with.

By going along with this new baby game and by inventing some telling variations of his own, Jean Piaget long ago mapped out one important turn of events during this first year: how babies come to appreciate the objective reality of things outside themselves. Piaget surmised that the young infant, when he turns his eyes from view to view, has no way of knowing whether his eyes are finding what is out there or whether he is creating the views by the act of looking. Piaget found very strong evidence that the infant does not live in an objective world where things exist even when he can't see them. Rather, he behaves as though he lives in a subjective world in which things appear through the power of his seeing. Only experience in watching and handling objects ultimately presses on him the knowledge that they have an independent existence at a distance from him even when he is not holding them in eye or hand, and this experience the baby actively seeks by changing the rules of the game.

As the game changes over the weeks to include objects brought into the relationship, which was formerly an end in itself, adults comply not only by providing objects but by presenting themselves as objects too. The baby's mother, a human object, at first probably has no more permanent a reality to her child than a rattle or a bottle. As the baby sees it, she exists at his command; when he wants her, she is there. They are, in effect, a single organism, with two parts acting in unison. Perhaps because of the intensity of this relationship, some researchers believe that a mother is the first object that does not vanish like the smile on the Cheshire Cat, that she is the first that can be out of sight but still in mind.

The baby is able to perform this crucial feat as his brain matures and becomes capable of representing, storing, and recollecting his mother's image. But he is also forced to do so by circumstance. His mother's appearances and the performances the baby expects do not always come off as immediately or as satisfactorily as the baby wishes. There are times when he is hungry and she is on the telephone, or he is ready to dance and she is tired of dancing. There is space between them and the baby begins to see they are not one person. So the baby magician forsakes one conjuring act—making Mother appear—by replacing it with another—making Mother up.

The baby's attempt to memorize his mother is not in the least bit subtle. His new game—we could call it Exploration—involves vigorous and persistent investigation of the "pieces" of his mother, her glasses, nose, hair, the inside of her mouth. Again, taking the cue in perfect time, mothers introduce their own variations on this theme of exploring bodies as objects: Pat-a-Cake, This Little Piggy, Show Me Your Nose, Soooooo Big, and most appropriately of all, Peek-a-Boo. It is as though they knew all along what the baby was up to, for sure enough at about seven months there comes a time when the baby—having spent much time nuzzling, patting, gazing, pinching, pulling, poking, and otherwise exploring his mother—has her sufficiently memorized to know who she is without repeated investigations. Typically, the game of Exploration is topped with a final variation in which the baby stems his arms and legs against his mother, pushing off from her body to gain perspective on her whole face. He has found what he was looking for: a memory, a mental image, a portable Mom.

Now the young director takes over the production of Peek-a-Boo. From enjoying the passive experience of his mother's disappearance and reappearance, the baby shifts the focus of the game by naïvely covering his own eyes with his hands to hide himself. Himself. By the time a child can play this advanced form of Peek-a-Boo, he has constructed not only a mental image of his mother but an image of his self. He may not yet recognize it when he sees it in the mirror, and he may not yet realize it is visible to others even when its own eyes are covered, but there is no doubt that this form of Peek-a-Boo can't be played without it.

Parents don't need to be told how rapidly the game continues to change during the remainder of a baby's first year. Soon the lap baby will slide down to play at his mother's feet, to crawl, to pull himself to a standing position, to take his first steps. The long series of transforming games infants play with us leads unerringly toward a separate self and those first baby steps of distance between us.

By the age of a year, girls do not yet prefer dolls to trucks, nor do boys spurn purses and perfume. But a girl's baby steps do not take her the same distance from her mother as a boy's. Girls stay closer, boys go further. That is what the floor-square measurers can see. But is the unseen self of one-year-old boys and girls different too, one closer to, the other farther from, the image of the mother with which it is now paired? All along we have had to infer from what we can see, looking from the outside for the internal patterns that might be represented by the games of infancy. As mothers and fathers play the game, what is the meaning of their contrasting styles and what does the baby make of them? And were the baby to be the opposite sex, would either parent play the game in quite the same way?

There is little research that can give us firm footing in this slippery terrain. At every step, we must weigh slim clues in the balance of our own insights and experience.

Studies of how mothers and babies negotiate their earliest social encounters seem to show that meshing, when it has worked smoothly, gives the mother a sense of almost perfect unity with her baby. Mothers of very young infants, up to a month or two old, find that leaving the baby worries them terribly no matter how tired they are or how badly they thought they needed time off. Sitting in a restaurant, taking in a movie, a mother feels as though she had left a part of herself behind.

Tronick's experimental work with fathers hints that fathers do not, at any point, experience their baby as part of themselves. Fathers in Tronick's studies stressed exciting unpredictability, whereas mothers played with smooth continuity, containing the baby and enfolding him within the confines of the game. Adults who can remember early play with their father recall the toss in the air, the swoop between the legs, breathtaking physical sensations that come back with a mixture of intoxication and apprehension. The most routine day, we notice with our own children now, is punctuated by one dramatic event: "Daddy's home!" (When a working mother walks through the door, she is more likely to receive the day's complaints from the children than a rousing cheer.) Rather than behaving in ways that might blur boundaries between parent and child, men behave in ways that make their "otherness" distinctive.

Our culture emphasizes the otherness of fathers by keeping men away from their children for many hours during the day. Most fathers therefore have less opportunity than mothers to keep up with the day-to-day quirks of their developing offspring and may have no choice but to respond to sons and daughters in less individualized ways. Conversations with the most liberated families reveal, however, that even when families try very hard to erase such distinctions, differences remain. A couple whose professions allow both the husband and the wife to work part time and share in child care has made some interesting observations. Regardless of the fact that each parent has had equal time with their baby and that the father has participated in every aspect of care, the mother notes that his "timing" is off, that he fails to pick up subtleties of mood or mesh his approaches to the child's moment-to-moment states of mind as easily as she does. She readily admits her husband is their child's preferred playmate. (This mother's observation should remind us that females do seem to notice, according to psychologists' research, a great deal of incidental detail. Detail may not be incidental where child-rearing is concerned.)

One overriding biological event may well contribute to a mother's connectedness to her infant and to a father's distance. Only mothers have the experience of pregnancy on which to pattern a sense of continuity with their baby. The new father has been a bystander to his wife's gestation and labor, and some men complain that they feel like bystanders after the baby is born, too. The father feels that he doesn't really know how to deal with diapers and burping, or he doesn't like baby noises, messes, and smells, or the baby is still too "fragile" for a man to handle comfortably. Quite commonly, a husband feels his wife and baby are involved with one another to his exclusion, so that instead of being raised to fatherhood, he is reduced to bachelorhood. This feeling rarely lasts very long, however, and by the time Tronick recorded their play style with their month-old babies, fathers have already slipped into their unique role as playmate.

The special quality of father-play that Tronick noticed when infants were only a month old continues in related forms as the child grows, and there is an increasing tendency for playfulness to color the most routine care giving between father and child. Mothers simply carry a tired toddler to bed; fathers piggy-back them. When two-year-old Anna awoke weeping from her nap and wanted her red socks put on, her father thanked her for the "mittens" and put them on his hands. Too cranky to appreciate the joke just then, Anna took the red socks to her mother. Susan's family has worked out an arrangement under which her working mother can sleep late Sundays while Susan's father cares for her. The weekly date takes Susan and her father first to buy the newspaper, then to have breakfast at a counter, then on a stroll around the village during which all sorts of small adventures are enjoyed. When they get home, Susan's mother changes her out of her pajamas.

Fathers often react, in amusing ways, to their babies more in terms of what they will (or should) become, while mothers deal with the here-and-now child. Fathers, not mothers, present their sons with mini-baseball shirts. One father tried to solve a playpen brawl by placing the two 30-pound combatants in opposite corners, a territorial compromise entirely beyond them. His wife handed out cookies. And it is fathers who preposterously introduce infants to ocean surf and horses' backs in preparation for their (distant) futures.

Women easily see their husband's antics with their child as a failure to mesh, but they may be missing the point. By behaving unpredictably and by offering a high level of stimulation, fathers may pose an important challenge to the infant's ability to respond to the unexpected and to regulate his own recovery from stress. The baby may be enticed by his father's antics to venture further outward into the world toward the absurd faces and funny noises that only Daddy makes. The big, wild swoops, the rougher skin and tighter grip, may help the baby better define the physical boundaries of his self. And as that self emerges, babies often approach their fathers with particular joy. Objecting to being manhandled by a mother who has not yet learned to respect his new independence, the baby may still welcome romping with his father, taking in by gulps the otherness and outside world he offers.

Remembering that evolution has probably equipped males to venture further from the home and that men of all known cultures involve themselves in the public aspects of human life, these observations should not surprise us. Fathers seem to represent the outside world to both sexes—its standards and expectations as well as its adventure and novelty.

The idea that mothers naturally sense a continuity with their babies that spans the disruption of birth and links passive care of the fetus with active care of the newborn baby is probably not quite accurate. Much as a woman may have the sense of knowing her baby before it is born, and may even give it a pet name, the baby who is actually born is a stranger she has never heard, seen, or touched before. This new baby is gained, but the other, inside baby—and many of the fantasies connected with it—is lost. The sense of loss combined with a low mood caused by normal hormonal goings-on and the very real stress of becoming a mother may contribute to the prevalence of postpartum blues. Most women are soon able to dispel their distress as they find new grounds for unity by feeding, holding, stroking, and even sniffing their newborn baby. (Interestingly, there is some recent evidence that adoptive mothers find the meshing process—the period of negotiation that has merging as its goal—somewhat more troublesome, although the difficulties can be overcome.) The sense of joyful completeness that is often attained defines our most fundamental idea of motherhood. We need not argue whether such unity and joy is natural, usual, or ever more than transient, but merely note that such a state is sought. When it does not come about, the mother is less than happy with this period of her life and the baby is faced with certain problems in separating from her. Since the same grounds for unity seem just as available to fathers, we should also remark the fact that fathers fail to report a comparable sense of bliss, although they certainly report excitement and delight.

The period of merging is in any case more complete and satisfactory to the baby than it is to the mother. Women have many connections with the outside world, whereas babies usually have no outside interests to speak of. We have seen that this period may be effortless or troublesome, depending on the match between mother and baby. We can guess that each partner's past history—the fact of prematurity, for example, or the way the mother was herself mothered—can affect the outcome too. Is the mother's sense of unity with her baby, or the quality of their mutuality, also affected by the baby's sex?

This interesting question has not been studied as it relates to the first year of a baby's life except indirectly and in retrospect, as it is revealed in clinical work. Even without examining detailed case histories, however, we can ask ourselves what we have felt and fantasized.

Many women claim that giving birth to a female baby seems perfectly natural, as though the female form is molded by the female form and that is what one expects to come out. To produce a penis—and the boy that accompanies it—is rather more incredible. When women ardently wish for a daughter in preference to a son, they tend to muse on the many experiences they will share, the thread of continuity from mother to daughter through the generations. One woman who has had only sons regrets never having had the pleasure a daughter could bring. She feels sons are for the world; she will lose them. A daughter would have been for her.

There runs through these musings a persistent awareness of a boy's essential difference from his mother and of a girl's essential similarity. The awareness came over one woman quite suddenly. Upon the birth of her second child, a boy, she was startled to discover a certain squeamishness about cleaning her son's penis during diapering, although she had felt quite natural about cleaning her daughter's genitals. She was, as she reports, "freaked out" to realize he—who had been part of her—was a member of the opposite sex.

Intuition suggests that this is where a mother's intense awareness of her baby's sex slips into place. Nancy Chodorow, an assistant professor at the University of California at Santa Cruz whose work has focused on the relationship between mothers and daughters, thinks that during the baby's months of psychological unity with his or her mother, the tenor of the duet is not quite the same for a boy as for a girl baby. Meshing must be "good enough" for a baby of either sex to develop in a healthy way, yet there is no prescribed intensity that it must achieve nor an exact length of time that it must last. There is leeway for quite a range of "good enough" meshing, and there is no reason to suppose any less leeway for the kind of selfhood a baby begins to sense. Differences in completeness or duration of a mother's and baby's unity could well be reflected in the kind of self the child experiences.

To whatever extent the mother experiences her baby as a separate person, different from or even in contrast to herself, to that extent might the baby experience himself as separate and contrasting, as is likely to be the case when the baby is a son. To whatever extent the mother experiences her baby as continuous with herself, joined and similar, to that extent might the baby experience herself as indistinct from her mother, blurred and permeable. This is more likely to be the case if the baby is a daughter.

We have seen that mothers of boys cater to them somewhat less than mothers of girls as early as three months of age, so boys may get not only a firmer, but also an earlier, push from the nest. For a boy, the sense of being an individual may emerge sooner and be more complete. For girls, attended to closely for a longer time, the sense of self may be less complete and emerge later.

Since not only the mother's feelings but also the baby's behavior influence their relationship, we must also look at the various sex differences Maccoby and Jacklin noted. Baby girls who particularly respond to touch invite cuddling. A boy baby's less interested response to touch may discourage his mother from cuddling him, but his greater imperviousness to rough handling—including his higher pain threshold—may invite a certain boisterousness. Girls might be helped to sustain a sense of partial fusion with their mothers if they are often stroked and cuddled, while boys, handled less and bumped about somewhat, may establish definite body boundaries earlier and more definitely than girls. The fact that girl babies tend to vocalize more and mothers to talk with them more provides another avenue for female continuity. All that chit-chat maintains contact between mother and daughter even when they are at a distance from one another. The girl's more frequent smiles are rewarding too, and mothers are known to look more often at their girl babies, perhaps to reap the delight of grins and coos. Looking, too, bridges the space that separates them. (With this in mind, we can appreciate that the "rejecting" mothers of Kagan's study might have failed to meet their daughter's cuddly expectations well enough, so that the little girls persisted in their efforts to achieve a closeness they never had. A boy baby whose mother was not so cuddly might have less difficulty enjoying distance, though there is plenty of evidence that neither sex comes through such failures unscathed.)

Energy levels probably play their part in this scheme, too. A mother would have to be a wrestler to hold on to certain male babies by the time they approach their first birthday, and some distance from a struggling body may come as a relief to both of them. Biology may also propel the infant boy further from his mother's side, increasing his perception of himself as separate and distant.

Thus even before the baby becomes recognizably masculine or feminine in any stereotyped way, differing experiences of some basic relationships have very likely led to differing kinds of self—on the one hand clearcut, hard-edged, and relatively impermeable, on the other blurred, diffused, and permeable. Children's future courses as they cope with the hard knocks of toddlerhood diverge in keeping with this fundamental and most important of sex differences. But not much is visible yet. Even the differences Kagan's group reported, which sound so striking when put into words, are not large when expressed as numbers. For example, the mean time spent banging toys during the whole fifteen-minute experiment was about twenty seconds for girls, about thirty-five seconds for boys. That is not a lot of bangs for either sex and not a lot more for boys than for girls. Such differences would be extremely difficult to notice without the help of floor squares, stopwatches, and key-punched notation.

Researchers themselves are handicapped without such tools. As Goldberg and Lewis ruefully admit in one report, "On some occasions, staff members have incorrectly identified the sex of an infant. Mothers are often clearly irritated by this error." They go on to remark that since "the sex of a fully clothed infant is difficult to determine, the mistake seems understandable and the mother's displeasure uncalled for."[2]

That difficulty will not be resolved until the child himself is adamant about his or her sexual identity, wants to wear pink, does not want to play with dolls, and in many other ways purposefully takes on the behavior that will inform the rest of the world of his or her gender. The one year old has not done that yet.

Gender is not an issue to the infant; his own development does not yet demand a gender identity. That will happen, and happen very rapidly, as the toddler deals with his knowledge of having a self and of being a separate person. The very rapidity with which the toddler assumes a gender and fills out the role implies that the way for it has been prepared in advance, and so solidly that within another year or so gender identity will be irreversible.

5

THE BIRTH OF
GIRLS AND BOYS

Elizabeth enjoyed her first birthday party immensely. Her cake was a nice brown chocolate, and all her guests received rubber ducks as favors. She was delighted with her pounding bench and stacking toys, including the pyramid of colored rings from Johnny, a cousin who was her own age. Johnny's party, to which Elizabeth was invited the next month, was about the same. His father hopefully gave him a plastic baseball bat, but Johnny banged it about the same way he did the stuffed doll his grandma gave him.

By their second birthdays Elizabeth's and Johnny's parties were totally different. Elizabeth's cake was now pink, although Johnny's was chocolate again. Elizabeth gave out little cars to her boy guests and small purses to the girls. But Elizabeth hardly played with her guests at all; she was too engrossed with her new baby doll. As soon as Elizabeth unwrapped her doll, she cradled it in her arms as if she had mothered babies all her life. She dressed it and undressed it; it could be washed and made to drink and pee. Johnny's grandmother wouldn't have thought for an instant of getting him a doll this year. A big red fire engine that squirted water when connected to a hose was more like it. One look at it, and Johnny was off to a fire.

Had Johnny's and Elizabeth's families suddenly turned sexist? Not at all. They, like most of us, were responding as usual to their powerful babies who, somewhere between their first and second birthdays, had informed their parents that they had become girls and boys. By the time children celebrate their second birthday, they have acquired a gender identity that will direct their inner lives and be the inextricable core of their sense of self throughout their lifetimes.

We know it when we see it. One day we look in amazement at our child and say, often aloud, "Look, he is a real little boy now." The fact that it takes us by surprise shows that we are mystified as to how this came about and do not really believe we have wrought the miracle in so short a time with the clumsy tools of training and example. Again, it is what the child brings to his or her own development, supported by our often unwitting responses to those expectations, that accounts for the startling emergence of masculinity and femininity we can plainly see in two year olds. We will have to backtrack a few months to pick up the thread of what happens during this amazing second year.

In the brief period between the age of seven months, when the baby first playfully hides his newfound self behind his pudgy hands, and one year, the baby's capacity to act independently accelerates dramatically. His ability to initiate his own plans of action escalates into what is probably the headiest exhibit of power a person ever projects. The baby stands, he walks. His mood appears so ecstatic that these months have been called the toddler's "love affair with the world." He behaves as though the world turns and moves for him, at once boundless and within his grasp. There is no limit to his adventures. He is elated all day and can hardly bear to give up his new powers in order to go to sleep at night. So charged with pleasure are his encounters with the insides of cupboards and the wide-open reaches of space that he is beyond frustration and nearly impervious to bumps and falls.

How exciting it must be, as the toddler's sturdy legs propel him into the first few months of his second year, to lift wastebaskets, smear cold cream, clomp about in rubber boots, grab a toy from another child, pull the cat's tail and make her squeal. The more the toddler discovers about his powers, the more expansive and grand is his image of himself. It balloons out so as to fill his head quite full of himself. Where is his mother? He doesn't know; he doesn't care. He hasn't even noticed that she is not at his side.

Up to this peak of omnipotence in an infant's development, gender has not been an issue. The one year old may be by nature already somewhat girlish or boyish (or neither, or the opposite of his or her actual sex). Early relationships with both parents may have shaped the young toddler's behavior in a way that adults are tempted to label masculine or feminine. Internally, too, the quality of merging may differ for male and female in intensity, completeness, and duration, and this has probably prepared the ground for later developments. But there is no evidence that gender has concerned the child or that being a boy or girl has played a part in his or her developing self-awareness. The baby's interests have been in moving out to greet his mother, moving out further to greet the world, and again moving on to become the agent of his own experience, a person on his own. All this he has done through a kind of subjective magic in which he has not grasped the reality of his physical separation from all other people or coped with the repercussions of that knowledge.

This baby, at somewhere around his first birthday, is poised on the brink of a great comedown. His happy state of ignorance cannot continue long. He is small, not really very powerful, and the world gradually reveals itself to be far more intractable than he had thought. Big pots will not fit into small ones, sidewalks scrape the knees and tables bruise the head. Eventually, the cat will turn and scratch and the other child will bop him one. The child's self-esteem deflates, and beyond his shriveled ego, the toddler discovers his mother where in fact she has been the whole time—at a considerable distance from his side.

It is not easy to understand how this can come as such a surprise. The explanation could be that the inner psychological distance between the infant and the mother is much shorter than the actual distance the walking child can now create between them. The toddler seems to assume his mother's closeness, as though she were as portable as her image. When he does get into trouble—bangs his head or stubs his toe—mothers may notice a puzzled expression just before the tears. The toddler had not realized his mother was not right there, sharing his adventure. Although they are represented as two individuals, in the child's mind they still experience the world in common and in tandem. (Remnants of that expectation are expressed for several more years in the child's conviction that his mother can read his mind, as though she really were inside it.)

The age at which this dawning occurs varies, so that one child's elated mood may deflate as early as a year, another's not until he is well into his second year, often depending on how early or how late the child experiences the exhilaration of learning how to walk. When it occurs, however, the toddler's deflation is quite visible.

At times a shadow of loneliness comes over the younger toddler even at the height of his love affair with the world, when he is about a year old. When a young toddler's mother leaves the room, her child's exuberant mood sinks visibly. He appears subdued, loses interest in whatever activity he was involved with, and appears to be concentrating on his own thoughts. Perhaps he is concentrating on the image of his mother, holding her in his mind when he cannot find her in the real world. Or again, in the midst of play, the toddler seems to run out of steam, to be unable to continue on his own. He seeks out his mother, briefly leans against her or lays his head in her lap. Then, after only seconds of contact, he seems to recover his energy completely and is off again. The young toddler's self-image seems to lack substance and energy; he partakes of his mother by intense imagining or by physical contact. Thus psychically refueled, he can fend off loneliness for short periods.

But by the time the toddler notices the actual distance that separates him from his mother, imagining and refueling are not enough. His previous imperviousness to bumps and his cheeriness even while attempting to cram the big pot into the small one dissolve. The bumps hurt him, the pots frustrate him; he cries in pain and anger. Just when parents have come to appreciate their one year old's new skill and independence, the toddler abruptly requires constant help, seems always underfoot, follows his mother's every step, and strongly objects to each leavetaking. Though he still adventures, he must share every new discovery with his mother, loading her lap with each new find or pulling at her to come see this, that, everything. He is relentlessly demanding.

No matter what she does, a mother can no longer satisfy her toddler. He cries and cries when she must leave him, and ignores her when she returns. He whines for help but then pushes her away, annoyed at his need, annoyed at her compliance, and still annoyed if she refuses. One particular game aptly expresses the child's predicament: eyes twinkling in anticipation, he darts full tilt away from his mother expecting that she will—as of course she does—pursue him and sweep him safely into her arms. We easily appreciate how dangerous a game this is when we remember the toddler's propensity for aiming himself toward streets and precipices; the game is one of inner danger, too. On the one hand, the child clearly wishes to be caught and safely enfolded; and on the other, he wishes to be free. What if Mommy didn't catch him and he were to continue off into the blue totally alone? Yet what if she caught him and were never to let go? The toddler wishes to go backward into infancy and forward onto childhood. And both directions are as frightening as they are compelling.

This new game of chase that toddlers initiate points also to the new sort of relationship the child has with his mother. The two are only occasionally now a single organism from which both wish and fulfillment appear to arise. More often, as the months pass, they are partners, the one dependent, the other dependable. In that sense, the two are by no means entirely disentangled. The toddler seems to hover in that space he himself creates between the child who chooses to leave and the mother who reliably retrieves him. Without his partner, the infant is still incomplete.

One repercussion of this new awareness of his need is that the baby comes to value his mother. We could say that love has begun. Now that the child perceives his mother as a permanent individual who, if not in the living room may be found in the kitchen, the toddler is assured that she will not vanish into thin air. There is no such assurance about her emotions. Her love can disappear, as indeed it seems to when the toddler gets into trouble with her. As his world diminishes in grandeur, and his self-esteem as well, he becomes especially aware of this new threat.

This particular worry signifies the specific task that now faces the toddler. To remain cheerful and to progress toward independence, the child must forge a trustworthy link of love across the gap that now separates him from his mother. He must not only represent himself and his mother as permanent individuals with lives of their own, but as permanently loving individuals whose mutual attachment can be relied upon to support the child as he faces the world on his own two feet. In short, the toddler's task, in spite of disappointment and the world's hard knocks, is to construct a good relationship with Mother.

From this precarious perspective, and no longer buoyed up by magic, the toddler faces the fact of his separateness. We can easily understand that it is a sobering experience. But it is more sobering for girls than for boys. Girls remain subdued for longer, they complain and cling more, and when they do find a way to assure a loving bond between themselves and their mother, it is by an altogether different route from the one boys discover.

Psychoanalysts, whose approach to child development is traditionally more sweeping than that of research psychologists, have long been interested in this period when an infant takes on an informed and purposeful gender identity. Foremost among those psychoanalysts who have made infancy their special field is Dr. Margaret Mahler, a professor emeritus at Albert Einstein College of Medicine and visiting professor at the Medical College of Pennsylvania. During the past several decades of her long professional life, Mahler has been studying healthy children in a natural setting at Masters Children's Center in New York; here she and her colleagues can observe mothers with their infants and toddlers over years of everyday life.

Mothers (or, on certain days, fathers) come to her each weekday morning and stay for several hours chatting with one another park-bench style, doing their own work, playing with their babies, caring for them, or just watching over them as they would at home or in a playground. Observers keep notes on what is occurring, in the center and also during home visits. In addition, Dr. Mahler and her coworkers film the children's behavior at intervals, and also bring in professional testers to provide individual profiles of each child at various stages of development.

All these techniques combine to give a detailed description of each child that begins when he is about three months old and continues until, at three years old, he leaves the center to enter nursery school. Compared to the methods used in most psychology research, which can be likened to still shots that preserve particular moments, this method creates an extremely long movie.

Dr. Mahler's "movies" have recorded many of the developments we have already noted: the coming apart of the infant's merging with his mother as he stems his arms and legs against her, the exuberance of his early toddling days, his tedious vacillation between "do it myself" and whining for help as he realizes his dependency, and his transient sadness. The wealth of detail and the depth of these observations have also recorded distinctions between boys and girls which, quite blurred during their first year, now begin to come into focus. Parents may notice the more apparent ones: the first signs of differing preferences in play and playthings. A two-year-old daughter may now prefer a doll to a stuffed dog; a two-year-old son discovers the joys of blocks and wheeled toys. But Mahler, with the advantage of studying many children, with many observers over many years, has noted a more subtle difference. The sobered mood characteristic of the child at about one and a half years old tends to be more pronounced in girls than in boys; nor do girls easily overcome their sadness. By eighteen months, Donna, who was the most competent, self-assured, and cheerful of all the toddlers in her group, cried easily when scolded and feared loud noises, as though they were scolding her too. Bruce, a serious little boy who did not meet the world with much exuberance, had managed to cheer himself up by nineteen months even though neither his temperament nor his personal history was so promising as Donna's.

Toddlers of both sexes, Mahler noted, gradually fend off the loneliness of being separate. In this they are aided by their own continuing development and by their parents' approval of their growing autonomy. Language helps, for the child now rapidly learns this long-distance way of keeping in touch, and so does physical competence. The sheer excitement of bumping down the stairs on the seat of their pants brightens their mood, and that is only one of an incredible array of skills that enables them to open, close, fit, push, stack, lift, leave, and return. Keeping busy, for the toddler as well as the adult, lifts the spirits.

The lift, however, seemed to Mahler to be greater for boys than for girls. There may be several reasons for this. The quality of the feats themselves appear to differ in boys and girls. Not only Mahler but most observers of children at this age are impressed with the push and thrust, the sheer tenacity with which the boy toddler tackles the world—as we have seen when, at the age of thirteen months, boys tried to tear down the barricade between themselves and their mother by brute force, while girls solved the problem in relational terms, by imploring their mother with gestures and tears. Similarly, when a mother leaves her toddler, closing the door behind her, both boys and girls may cry and linger at the door, but it is the boys who tend to get in a few good kicks and bangs at the door while they're at it.

Boys protest interference with their autonomy, too. They are more likely than girls to duck a kiss, squirm out of a hug, refuse to hold hands or lay still for diapering. Teachers in day-care centers notice that although both sexes attempt to yank a toy from another child's grasp, boys persist in this effort and succeed more often than girls. Girls yank, but at the same time their eyes are often seeking the teacher's help.

Greater strength and aggression must certainly contribute to the boy's spirit-lifting tenacity, but his inner relationships must color this period too. His greater inner distance from his mother is reflected in the actual distance he keeps from her as he plays. Many toddlers set off toward their mothers to check in with her after they have played at a distance for a while, only to veer away at the last moment as though they had suddenly changed their minds and prefer their independence after all. This "just checking" behavior, Mahler observed, is more common in boys than in girls, who tend to continue their course straight to their mother's lap.

There is a possibility not only that the firmness of a boy's self-image and his resulting self-esteem help him to maintain distance, but that built-in and seemingly unrelated tendencies feed into this specific ability. If boys find it easier to grasp the ins and outs of space, they may be better able to represent their mother's whereabouts, maintaining a stable and reliable image toward which they can remain oriented even when she is not nearby. They may feel more convinced of their control over distance, able both to venture farther from their mother's side and to retrace that path when necessary.

Finally, mothers may respond rather differently to independence and prowess depending on whether their child is of the same or opposite sex. Often a mother can't help applauding—sometimes by literally clapping—what she perceives to be her son's maleness as he leaps from a step, hauls a suitcase, roars like an airplane down the hall. These exhibitions, she may feel, are not to be tampered with or tempered by too much civilizing. Also, such behaviors are rather out of the female line, the bravado foreign though pleasing.

Girls of the same age are not without showiness, but when they jump up and down on a bed in breathless excitement, the mother is more likely to appreciate the activity through identification rather than admiration, to approve but not to applaud. (This subtle difference is not easy to grasp. Parents of teenagers may be able to imagine it by recalling their own imagery as they fantasize their children's futures. In such fantasies, a mother tends to position herself as the observer as her son becomes this or that. When imagining her daughter's future, she participates in the imagery as if the events were happening to herself. Boys are the objects of their mother's fantasies; girls are the subjects of their mother's fantasies.)

For all these reasons, both physical and psychological, the boy toddler ultimately relates to his mother *at a distance from* and *in contrast to* her. This break from identification with his mother—with femaleness—we can consider the core of masculinity. And masculinity is, in turn, the key to the boy's resolution of the separation crisis. He comes to love his mother as a member of the opposite sex.

Such a break isn't totally possible for girls. A girl can't forge a completely separate identity from her mother by grasping at the contrast between them because there is too little contrast. It is barely experienced, seldom emphasized, and never applauded. The girl's biological gifts strengthen rather than weaken continuity as she sticks close to her mother, exchanges glances, and weaves her web of sounds and smiles. She feels the impact of the outside world less sharply simply because she doesn't thrust herself so hard upon it. The girl's inner distance is perhaps never great; she remains open to a sense of continuity with others and doesn't sense a sharp boundary that marks where she leaves off and others begin. This sense of continuity we can consider the core of femininity. When faced with separation, the girl finds herself *close to* her mother and *similar to* her. Although the girl, too, achieves a bond of love with her mother, her course is marked by ambivalence, and the issue of separation is not entirely resolved.

The events in a toddler's life we have looked at so far, those that occur up to nineteen or twenty months, still do not support the extraordinary vigor with which girls now begin to cuddle with their dolls and boys to shun dolls for tractor trailers—to take on the unmistakable colors of their gender roles. For instance, boys may now quite suddenly show an intense identification with their father as they begin to drape themselves with neckties, stomp about in their father's shoes, and squirt shaving cream on their own baby faces. A boy not only displays difference from his mother; the differences he chooses are distinctively masculine. The explanation seems obvious: he has discovered the fact of his gender.

At some time during this second year—for boys even earlier—toddlers begin to integrate into their self-image the bodily signs of gender their parents so eagerly noted at the moment of their birth. This includes not only how their genitals look, but also the sensations that arise from them. Soon toddlers will begin to notice the difference between their genitals and those of the opposite sex. That blow to innocence is what fuels their pursuit of a gender identity. How toddlers deal with the physical nature of their sex and with their knowledge of the difference between boys and girls alters the course of their development dramatically and, in fact, cements the differences between the sexes.

Baby boys discover their genitals as early as three or four months of age, and not later than a year. Between seven and ten months, most have come upon their penis in the course of happy slappings and clutchings at their body during diapering and bathing. At first, a boy's handling of his genitals does not appear to be erotic. Although a baby boy's penis becomes erect when his bladder is full, infants under a year rarely get erections from touching their genitals or by having them touched. From outward behavior, it appears that discovering the penis has no greater significance than discovering ears or toes.

Equal status for body parts is not, however, granted for long. Within a few months the penis's potential for pleasure distinguishes it from other body parts and comes to interest the child particularly. As events of the second year show, the boy becomes aware that his penis is important to hang on to both physically and psychologically.

Certain interesting features of male genitals become apparent to the baby boy as soon as he learns to pull himself to a standing position. Now, by leaning his head down to peer beyond his protruding belly, he can clearly see what he had only gropingly felt before. His penis sticks up, it flops down; it has a life of its own. Shortly after he had learned to toddle on his own, Sam sat diaperless on the floor repeatedly pushing his erect penis down as he sternly commanded "No!", only to smile as it popped up again and again.

The penis is not only an amusing Jack-in-the-box, it is a water pistol. The boy soon finds he can squirt a stream of urine from his penis, and this stream he himself can turn on and off. Boys typically begin to take pride and pleasure in their urinary accomplishments sometime during the first few months of their second year. This interesting subject leads them to become curious about other people's bodies. They pull the pants off dolls, lift skirts, reach for women's breasts. Fascinated, they follow their mother and father into the bathroom to watch them urinate. Their eyes are glued particularly on their father's dramatic performance: the strong stream, loud splashing, and many bubbles men make. Some boys reach to touch the stream or even attempt to mouth it.

The interest of boy toddlers soon extends to their father's penis, too, which may be gazed at or grabbed for, and also to any salient features that mark possessors of penises. Jeff, one subject in a particularly thorough study of this period by Eleanor Galenson and Herman Roiphe, psychoanalysts in the Department of Child Psychiatry at the Albert Einstein College of Medicine, is typical.

Jeff had been very interested in his father's urination since he was fourteen months old. By fifteen months he often drew his own and others' attention to his penis by pointing to it and pulling at it. Within another three months, at a year and a half, Jeff had developed a special relationship with his father, preferring to kiss him (as he became reluctant to kiss or cuddle with his mother) and to be sweetly obedient to him, although his father was not at all strict. All the while he remained extremely interested in his father's urination. At nineteen months, when allowed a "naked time" each evening, he dashed about in a showy fashion, often stopping for a delighted look at his own penis. By then, Jeff and his father had invented many roughhousing games to play together.

All this male mutuality resulted, by twenty months, in evidence of Jeff's identification with his father. While his father was at work, Jeff would recreate the horse-and-rider game they often played together by taking his father's role as horse. He mimicked his father's facial expressions and mannerisms, even to counting on his fingers as his father did and tinkering with the stereo equipment. A few months before his second birthday, Jeff proudly urinated in a standing position just like Daddy.

This urinary route to male identification is intense, and it remains a source of mutual pride among boys throughout their childhood. David and Danny, brothers one year apart, often went to the toilet together when the younger was not yet three. After gleefully shouting "Cross swords!" each aimed his stream of urine to intercept the other's stream. Joshua remembers that his father used to dig two holes, a larger and a smaller one, in the gravel driveway. Into these two holes father and son would simultaneously urinate. Interestingly, this incident appears to be a fantasy in retrospect, for Joshua's father recalls no such event. But fantasy or fact, such urinary tales are ubiquitous among boys.

Urinary sensations are not the only ones that seem to become central to the boy's perception of his body during the second year. Indeed, everything "down there" now seems to make itself felt in pleasurable ways. When little, the child merely grunted and concentrated during defecation; now he gets a dreamy look on his face as he has a bowel movement, often choosing to have it at some preferred time when he is relaxed and undisturbed by outside events. Just as his interest in urination now opens up new avenues of play—spitting, spraying the hose, turning faucets on and off, splashing in the bath—he begins to show that feces have become valuable to him. Almost every parent has had to clean up after at least one episode of feces smearing, ruefully noting the contrast between his or her exasperation and the child's delight. If parents are spared this, they nevertheless see their child's new interest by the way he smears his food, sloshes in the toilet, decorates himself with mud, or grovels about in the garbage pail. In keeping with his emerging sense of self and the value he now places on that self, he is attached to every bit of him, whether it's a part or a product of his body.

The genital and excretory organs and products are subject to curious appearances and disappearances. The boy's penis goes up and down, his testicles descend and retract, his urine stops and starts, his feces stay in, come out, and become detached. No child remains unaware of these events: in fact, the separation anxiety caused by his mother's appearances and disappearances may even make him notice them more acutely. Parents report that toddlers often object to having their dirty diapers changed, preferring to walk about with loaded pants no matter how adamantly adults disagree. The child's feces are his; he made them, and he doesn't want to part with them. Nevertheless, they are taken away. Even before they are flushed down the toilet, they are detached from the child's body. They are a valued part of him that, to his dismay, comes off.

The fact that feces are a "losable" item distresses a boy no less than a second shocking discovery during this period in his life. As noted, a boy's interest in urination leads him to follow both parents into the bathroom to watch how they perform. Rather quickly, however, the boy's interest in watching his mother urinate tends to fade. He may accompany her to the bathroom only to distract himself with wastebaskets and toilet brushes, or even distract her from her goal by running off with her lipstick or the roll of toilet paper she must then retrieve. But he does his best not to see what he has already observed: his mother does not have a penis.

Up to this point, the child has developed the psychological roots of gender identity, but not until he discovers the anatomical basis for being a girl or a boy can we say that he is aware of the implications of being one sex or the other. This fact of life now comes flying to the fore and becomes a matter of great concern, especially as, at about the midpoint of a boy's second year, his penis begins to afford him frankly sexual pleasure. During diapering now, he will often reach for his penis, fondle it, giggle, and invite his mother to share his pleasure with a glance and a smile. He mothers himself too, tenderly powdering his own penis or sudsing it in the bath. These ministrations frequently result in an erection. By the second half of the second year we must clearly label genital arousal erotic.

The coming together of all these developments during so brief a time in the child's second year creates a specific problem for the boy toddler. Just when he has come to value his penis for the feats it performs and the sensuous pleasures it affords, it occurs to him that his feces, located so close by, are detachable and that his mother, so close to him emotionally, lacks a penis altogether. Do penises, then, come off?

At this age, clinical evidence suggests that little boys are not at all convinced that their penises are firmly attached. You often see boys pulling at their penises with a concentrated air of experiment. One toddler, inspired perhaps by the disappearing act of his testicles as they retracted beyond his scrotum, pushed his penis into the surrounding flesh until it was completely inside. Jeff invented a new game to play with his mother. He pulled his hands up inside his sleeves. His mother said, "Where are your hands?" Gaily, Jeff thrust his hands out from beneath his cuffs. They played this reassuring game many times. Jeff also dealt astutely with his concern for losing small parts by becoming an avid rock collector at the tender age of twenty months. Many toddlers develop a sudden and overriding interest in belly buttons, an appurtenance that has the virture of being the same on both sexes. It is also quite common for the boy to give up masturbation for a while, as though the very pleasure were too great a reminder of the sexual difference.

More surprising than the male toddler's concern about the possibility of losing his wonderful penis is how mild that concern is. Unlike the anxious drama that will unfold a year or so in the future, the male toddler wastes little time in worrying. Those symptoms that are noticeable (they are not always noticeable) are usually relaxed and transient, mere ripples in the stream of progress. Indeed, the little boy, although concerned and displeased about the sexual difference he has observed, seems promptly to ignore it. He reacts the same way that he reacted to his mother's disappointing performance—he simply looks away.

A little boy supports this grand denial by emphatic masculinity. Trucks excite him; so do guns. And if he doesn't have one of these pushy objects, he just becomes one. "Brrrrrooooooom!" He is an airplane. He flies across the grass. Up, up he goes, zoomed high in Daddy's arms almost to the sky. Inanimate objects and the boy's whole body are used as though they were phalluses. Thus by naïve exaggeration the child hangs on to his newfound body image.

The hasty edifice of plunging trucks, squirting guns, and flying toddlers would surely collapse were it not that reality to some extent supports the little boy's newfound maleness.

Although Daddy may be the most ordinary man to us, to his son he is large, strong, deep-voiced, and acrobatic. He climbs ladders, makes big noises with a hammer, pumps gas into the car, and lifts little children to delirious heights. Identification with him and other males gives the boy an internal sense of participation in their strength and showiness. Comically and endearingly, the boy assures himself of his important similarity to Daddy by literally stepping into his shoes.

Then, too, the toddler is not yet experienced enough to take his observation of his mother's or another female's lack of a penis as the last word on the subject. Who knows, perhaps her penis is very small and will get bigger if she takes her vitamins every day. Mark reassured his mother that her penis would grow if she finished all her cereal. Or the penis may be inside and will come out when she wants it to. Based on the boy's very limited knowledge of growth, birth, and bowel movements, such things seem possible at this age. It will be many years before the child realizes that sexual difference is unalterable.

Most important, however, the boy's own penis is available for investigation at any time. Jeff played hide-and-seek with his penis, sucking in his rotund belly to catch a glimpse of it, relaxing his belly to make it disappear, sucking in again for a reappearance. He had only to look; it was always there.

For all these reasons a boy's discovery of the sexual difference augments masculinity in a way that fits smoothly with his efforts to separate from his mother. Shocking as the discovery is, it provides him with a further impetus not to identify with her, to seek a better distance from her. Further, feats of independence can now be equated with masculinity, so that the boy's thrusting out into the world takes on a specifically male significance. As luck would have it, his mother seems to admire just the tactic he has taken. Masculine behavior becomes a crucial ingredient in his general wooing of her love.

Looking at the year between the boy's first and second birthdays, an observer is more impressed with the progressive nature of his development than with its intermittent setbacks. In short, his mood is upbeat.

The same period is more troublesome for girls. Timing differs, and so does the eventual outcome. The baby girl doesn't discover her genitals until several months later than the average boy—usually at about one year. When she does, the discovery is pleasant but undramatic. There is nothing to grab hold of, there are no tricks to watch. From her viewpoint, peering over her tummy, there is not even much to see. Although physiological maturation dictates that she, like a little boy, begin to appreciate urinary sensations and achieve increasing control over her flow of urine, the source of the wonderful stream is hidden and the angle of flow rules out any show-off antics. The relationship between sensations arising in the urethra and those arising in the genitals cannot be visually investigated, nor is there a single organ invested with both phallic and urinary pride. The vagina, although it too contributes pleasurable feelings, is not available for inspection at all.

In terms of outward behavior, toddler girls in many ways resemble toddler boys. They, too, enjoy touching their genitals, and just as both sexes woo their mother by sharing with her each new object they come upon, both sexes first direct genital pleasure toward their mother, seeming to expect that she will appreciate or even participate in this early, relaxed form of masturbation. As a little girl's genitals become increasingly capable of sexual feeling, she also enjoys such sensations as swooping, spinning, and jumping up and down, or even more frankly sexual stimulation such as "riding horsey." Girls are every bit as interested as boys in smearing feces or messing in their spinach. And girls, too, follow their parents into the bathroom. They are just as shocked to discover the sexual difference.

The comparison between boys and girls can be pushed somewhat further, but not much. Like the boy, the girl believes in the potential detachability of penises, but in her and her mother's case, detachment may have occurred in the past rather than remain a threat in the future. If this thought is not to her liking, the girl can resort to the same naïve hopes as the boy: her penis (perhaps actually her clitoris) is small but will grow, is inside but will push out. Martha, who for months had needed her bottle only to fall asleep at night, began to demand it constantly. She often strutted about with her bottle between her thighs, nipple pointed outward, or sucked on her bottle while squeezing out the chubby flesh on her belly into a satisfactory protuberance. More usually, girls at first concentrate less on trying to grow a penis than on denying the sexual difference in much the same way boys do by such ploys as an exaggerated interest in the egalitarian belly button.

For such denial, however, the girl lacks support. Cathy, one of the girls in Mahler's study, was forced to notice that her little boyfriend had "two belly buttons." Taking a shower with her mother, Cathy grabbed at her pubic hair apparently looking for a hidden penis. But no matter how she tries, a little girl can't avoid the present reality of her life. She does not have a penis. Mahler's and many others' careful observations of girls in their second year of life reveal that as each comes upon evidence for the sexual difference, usually by twenty months of age, each inevitably reacts with disappointment. The reaction may be mild or it may be severe, but it is always noticeable, whereas the boy's discovery may easily pass unnoticed. Cathy, a charming, feminine, and precocious little girl, whom Mahler described as "everybody's favorite and a great comfort to her mother," changed abruptly. Before her discovery of her friend's "two belly buttons," she had enjoyed using the toilet. Now she refused to sit on it, whined, and held on to her genitals. Before she pulled at her mother's pubic hair in search of a penis, Cathy had been sweet with her playmates. Now no one could deter her from her particular form of aggression: hair pulling.

Probably both boys and girls experience a sense of loss as they conclude there are two sexes and they are only one of them. We will examine later the cognitive course of that realization and will see that for quite a while children view themselves as equipotential and do not necessarily believe their sexual condition is permanent. If the sense of loss were merely intellectual, however, both sexes should be equally disappointed to have only half of what they might have had, and both sexes should equally envy what the other possesses. But clinical evidence is clear on the matter. Girls are more disappointed than boys.

Adults often find it difficult to accept that all girls should originally see their genitals as lacking something. Why doesn't a girl feel as natural a delight in her genitals as a boy does in his? To grasp a toddler's emotions, we have to think in very childish ways. Red is better than brown because it is bright. Given the choice, very few children would choose dull brown shoes over shiny red ones. Adult aesthetics simply don't apply. Genitals that stick out and do tricks are better than ones that are flat and unskilled.

Girls can, of course, look forward to growing breasts and babies—feats boys do often envy—but to a child, these far-off events are every bit as likely as the prospect of growing a penis. Although both boys and girls consider all such stunning appurtenances possible for both sexes, at the moment the boy has something the girl has not. Recalling how difficult it is to convince a toddler to wait while we finish a two-minute telephone call, we can appreciate that expecting our daughter to wait patiently a dozen years for signs of womanhood is expecting too much.

The little girl is at a great disadvantage in even forming a clear idea of what and where her genitals are. Sensations arise over an ill-defined area that includes the clitoris and the vagina, possibly even the uterus. Most of that area is hidden away from both visual and tactile exploration. A girl may respond to sensations arising in her genitals by fondling her pubic area, but there is no way she can make anything change in size, shape, and consistency—that's for boys. Diffuseness blurs the distinction between genital, anal, and urinary sensations, and although the boy, too, is quite confused about which feelings and functions are assigned to which organs, he can check for misperceptions more easily.

Infant boys discover their genitals at a time when they are discovering other body parts as well, and are beginning to integrate all those bumps and hollows into a bodily image of themselves. The girl's discovery of her genitals is months later than the boy's discovery of his, so that her formulation of her bodily scheme is well along before she has any information with which to integrate the genital area. Even then, the information is far from complete. Her genitals tend to remain unclear to her even into adulthood. Thus both the girl's genital anatomy and the timing of her discovery compound her sense of lacking something, for she cannot easily focus on what it is she does have. Unlike the boy, she has nothing to hang on to.

Who is to blame for the little girl's sorry state? Her mother.

However idyllic a little girl's relationship with her mother has been up to this point, she now turns to her mother helplessly—and turns on her angrily, both clinging and coercing. She wilts and leans against her mother, whines, tugs her skirts, collapses in her lap. She issues orders and criticizes the results. To some extent such ambivalent behavior, babyish one moment and bossy the next, is characteristic of the separation process anyway, but with the revelation about the sexual difference, the girl's mood becomes more extreme. Her disappointment is palpable. She acts more helpless than can possibly be the case, more dissatisfied than appears reasonable, more accusatory than circumstances seem to warrant. Beneath the surface turmoil runs that undercurrent of sadness Mahler notes. Her mother hasn't given her what was surely in her power to grant.

If the little girl's conclusions are unreasonable, they are nevertheless comprehensible. Mother and daughter have until very recently been an omnipotent duo who could both wish and fulfill in harmonious unison. Their unity may have been more intense than a son's and his mother's. Their extrication one from another has not been so complete and so early. A little girl does not experience herself as totally separate, nor does she perceive her mother as having a real life of her own. There is some place in which the two remain one and from which the mother can still act as an omnipotent extension of the girl's own, rather small self. A girl may realize her own toddler limitations, but she still expects great things of her mother. We can imagine that if the girl has brothers—especially if a brother is born during this period— the girl has all the more reason to assume that women have the power to give and to withhold penises.

But even when this is not the case, girls blame their mothers for their "defect." (This may be as much an intellectual limitation as a psychological one. Up to five or six years old, children of both sexes lack the concepts of accident and coincidence. Everything that happens has to be somebody's fault.) The lack of a penis is treated by the little girl as though it were an unsettled debt. The mother "owes" the child something, if not a penis, then the red shoes and no substitute, right now and not later. This attempt to coerce her mother into acting as the little girl's omnipotent extension is only one aspect of a complicated cluster of emotions. Here is this child, in the midst of the normal deflation of toddlerhood, now faced with the final puncture in her self-esteem. From this low point, the happy time of babyhood before all this knowledge spoiled things looks pretty good. The girl begins to long for the good old days, and her longing propels her closer to her mother again, so that at the same time she finds fault with her mother, she is thrown back into her arms. The more severe the girl's reaction to the sexual difference, the more angry she will be and yet the more attached she will remain. Mother is the desert; mother is the oasis.

Boys also hold a grudge against their mothers, but it is less specific and there is a way around it. The grudge is closely related to the girl's. Both at first see their mothers as a derivation of the once-omnipotent self and therefore as omnipotent. Both experience that omnipotence as making them, by comparison, impotent—a feeling that is, of course, in accord with how suddenly helpless they feel as they begin to comprehend their limitations. And both blame their mothers for their impotence, as though she alone, and not the child too, had withdrawn from their initial unity and no longer allowed the child to share her power. However, for boys that grudge remains a general one, which is counteracted by their knowledge of having something different and desirable and by the reality of advancing skills, whereas the girl attaches blame to the specific circumstance of her defective body and often even retreats from real-life progress. Her impotence strikes her as concrete, provable. Therefore, her ambivalence toward her mother is greater than the boy's.

Mothers of daughters may recall this frustrating and tiresome time. Donna, whose competence and even-going cheerfulness had so impressed Mahler's group, seemed to become aware of the sexual difference at about eighteen months, when she was often observed lifting her skirt to study her own belly. Her easy, self-assured relationship with her mother became strained. When they were together, Donna bossed her mother around, telling her what to do and how to do it. When they were apart, Donna couldn't think of anything to do. When they were reunited, Donna needed to sit in her mother's lap and cling to her, only to whine and fuss and again command and coerce. It doesn't help a mother's self-esteem that just as her daughter is giving Mommy such a hard time, she begins to get along particularly well with Daddy.

Like the little boy, the girl toddler finds relief in her father. Her relationship with him has not arisen from an original unity and therefore her individuality is not threatened by closeness to him. He is powerful, but not omnipotent in the sense her mother had been, first in unison with her daughter and now in potential opposition to her toddler's independence. Daddy has always stood for autonomy. His earliest play encouraged his daughter to respond to the unexpected, to exercise controls that were not as necessary with her mother's smoother, more accurately modulated and more temperate play. Now he also stands for that freedom from her mother that the possession of a penis seems to confer.

Further, her father offers just the items of self-esteem the girl now badly needs, for he is more likely than her mother to bring such exciting and novel phenomena as flashlights and smoke rings to her attention, to encourage daring motor skills and to present a technical perspective on the world of objects. In many homes, the father is the "fixer"—perhaps a coincidental but still a compelling comparison with mother, the damager. So the little girl commonly turns to her father as a fixer of her psychological and (to her) physical injury. They form an alliance through which the girl hopes to achieve freedom.

Yet the relationship between father and daughter seldom takes on the intensity of the relationship between father and son at this age. Perhaps this is partly so because the penis and urinary act cannot serve as a focus, except insofar as the acquisition of a penis from her father seems focal to the girl; but a more telling perspective includes the girl's special relationship with her mother. Even as she moves toward her father, she is forever looking back at her mother.

The boy can use his identification with his father as a route to his mother's love. Masculinity gives him the independence and distance from her that autonomy requires but at the same time defines an opposite sex relationship to her. He becomes closer to his father, and from that position of strength renews his courtship of his mother. Rather early on, the boy's love relationships within the family form a triangle in which his father and his mother are nearly equally important. By comparison the discovery of the difference between the sexes creates special obstacles for the girl and very much prolongs the period during which she remains tied to her mother. Even well past a girl's second birthday, she may still be so ambivalently tied to her mother that there is barely room for her father to slip in edgewise. Her mother remains the girl's first and greatest love. Her approaches to her father may have a hint of seductiveness and intimacy, and their alliance does help to free her from her mother, but closeness to her father does not provide special access to her mother. At two and a half, Donna showed she wanted to be like Daddy by trying to imitate the way he urinated, by pointedly sliding a truck down an incline board between her legs, and even by openly proclaiming her belief that her penis would one day grow. But such proclamations did nothing to secure her mother's love. The most promising path to her mother is, of course, identification. Yet identification throws the girl into conflict: the more similar she is, the less free she feels; and the more she acknowledges her femaleness, the less she can hope for a penis.

As much as Donna's—and other little girls'—conflict seems unfortunate and unfair, it may represent a sine qua non of mature feminine identification. There is a paradox a girl must resolve. She already shares an identity with her mother in the infant's sense, and this primary identification is so deeply embedded as to be almost organic. To make a purposeful identification—to choose, as the boy does, to mimic and to incorporate admired traits of the loved person—she must first loosen her primary feminine identification and give herself some distance. Her very railing against her female state may do just that. Angry criticism of her mother may give the little girl the impetus to push herself away, to be her own kind of person—indeed, to be a better mommy than the one she has. Just as Donna was becoming most forthright in her pleading for a penis, she began to find another way to independence and love. From being Mommy's baby, she became a mommy to her own baby dolls and, in a sense, to herself as well. Rather pointedly, girls at this stage choose ways in which they do want to be similar to their mothers and ways in which they don't. Susan wanted to bake cookies for her friends and herself—just like Mommy—but became cantankerously opposed to the frilly clothes her mother wore and had preferred for Susan, too. Mothers who respect such choices begin to find their relationship with their daughters easier. Rather than shake our head over girls' pathetic hopes, we might better applaud their spirit. Were girls to have no argument with their mothers, their feminine gender identity might remain that of a baby's at the cost of their individuality and of their freedom.

Nevertheless, the girl's identification with her mother is not quite comparable to the boy's identification with his father. For the girl, being female will always retain elements of her primary relationship with her mother, so that besides wanting or choosing to be similar to her, she will feel herself and her mother to be the same in fundamental ways. Many women experience this remnant of oneness with their mothers quite consciously when they themselves become mothers. Distance shrinks, differences dissolve. They are converged in motherhood.

The developmental paths of boys and girls, so similar during the first year that there was little outward sign of difference, have by the end of their second year diverged in important ways, and will become even more strikingly different over the next several years. Standing back for a minute to view developments in the context of the child's wooing of his mother's love, we can see that each sex is by now inclined toward a least risky path.

Remember the characteristic game the toddler plays, darting away from Mommy, risking the danger of separation from her while courting the safety of her arms? What was a game to the toddler is not amusing to the two year old, for now closeness increasingly threatens the autonomy demanded by maturity, while full independence still seems— and is!— unthinkable. Closeness and independence both have their risks for both sexes, but the dangers of each differ for boys and girls. Were the boy to yield to his longing to re-merge with his mother, he would have to give up not only his autonomy but also his masculine identity, for that identity is predicated on distance, difference, and independence from her. While a girl has as much reason to fear remaining or becoming a passive extension of her mother, her feminine identity is predicated on her similarity to her mother and is therefore not at stake. Rather, it is distance, difference, and independence that may threaten to cut her loose and sever the basis of her bond with her mother.

These differences are not absolute. Both boys and girls value their autonomy even as they long for merging. Yet the emphasis on one risk over the other gives a gender-tinged shading to the problem of separation. As long as the boy feels safely independent, he can achieve a reliable attachment. As long as the girl feels attached, she can achieve a reliable independence. The least risky path for the boy, then, is to court his mother from the vantage point of independence, while the least risky path for a girl is to court her mother from the vantage point of dependence. This is not to say that there are any actual differences in independence and passivity between the sexes, but only that the children's *appeals* to their mother's love are likely to emphasize the one or the other according to the child's developing gender identity.

Mothers themselves can be expected to respond differentially to the wooing of a son or a daughter and also to react to the increasing sexuality of their offspring. A mother is bound to notice her year-old son when, with an inviting air, he intentionally reaches for and handles his penis, obviously for erotic pleasure. Erections may easily occur when a mother handles her son's genitals during diapering and bathing. It's hard to imagine a woman whose interest would not be at least mildly aroused and who would not appreciate her son in a somewhat sexually colored fashion. By comparison, sexual arousal in a baby girl is more clandestine, less visually seductive, easier to ignore, and without heterosexual overtones.

This subtle difference in the mother's reaction to her child's sexuality feeds into a tendency to ascribe contrasting significance to identical events. The mother is likely to see a son's wooing as a courtship, a daughter's wooing as a bid for closeness. While both son and daughter may drive the mother up the wall with their ambivalence and negativism, a mother's reaction to rebuffs may be colored with some admiration for her son's independence from her, some misgivings about her daughter's rejection of her.

Fathers, too, can be expected to respond to the changes in their children. We have already seen how male urination provides an avenue toward mutual identification between father and son, and how this is elaborated as fathers take upon themselves the masculine education of their sons. But they are not standing idly by as their daughters develop. As Donna became increasingly ambivalent toward her mother, she wanted her father to put her to bed, and when both her parents were going out together, she kissed her father but not her mother. A father said of his daughter at about this age: "I notice her coyness and flirting, 'come up and see me sometime' approach. She loves to cuddle. She's going to be sexy—I get my wife annoyed when I say this."[1] The comment is typical of fathers, and women report that their husbands hold out for long hair and dresses for their daughters, even when they themselves don't think it particularly important for a girl to look dainty at the age of two. Parents of both sexes, then, playfully ease their sons and daughters toward the heterosexual significance of gender identity.

That Elizabeth passes her second birthday in a psychological stalemate that seems gloomy compared with Johnny's cheerfulness should not divert us from the fact that neither sex has solved the problem of separation yet. While many boys may appear to have shrugged off their difficulties by turning toward their father, ignoring mother and denying her lack of a penis is hardly a promising tactic. Nor can the girl remain forever in that uncomfortable limbo of ambivalence. Both have to push onward.

6

A CHILD FALLS
IN LOVE

Martha, Lisa, and Jane haunt the dress-up corner in nursery school where they are involved in a complicated drama that requires memorized lines ("You say, 'Quick, run before the lion gets you,' and I'll say, 'No, I'll turn him into a kitten with my magic wand' "), numerous characters (including stuffed animals and dolls as well as themselves), and a host of real and imaginary props.

The girls have let Edward be the lion, but only as long as he consents to turn into a kitten. Failing to get the fun of this game and unwilling to be transformed into a kitten by a girl with a magic wand, Edward rejoins his pals, still a lion. The boys all begin a game of roaring. Notably absent from their performance are the rehearsed lines, the variety of characters, and the props. Indeed, the roaring game lacks any visible story line, although the lions do begin to prowl and stalk other children until the whole game gets out of hand and the teacher breaks it up.

The teacher rarely has to break up the girls' activities— Martha and her friends are by now caring for a substitute kitten who had been wrongfully changed into a lion by a witch. The girls stick closer to their teacher, ask for her help more often, and look to her for approval of their work and play. These are permanent traits. "Goodness" will be even more noticeable during elementary school, when girls stand for neatness, niceness, quietness, and studiousness and boys are known for their rowdiness and sloppiness. The girls' greater verbal ability, perhaps always more advanced than the boys', is now particularly obvious in the three-year-old girl's ability to freely symbolize, richly fantasize, and imaginatively pretend her way into many roles and tell rather long and intricate stories. That, too, is permanent. Edward, at fifteen, will complain with disgust about the endless personal journals some of his female classmates routinely produce. He simply will not be able to understand how they can have so much to say about their inner lives.

Parents of three year olds often remark that their sons are straightforward to the point of simplicity; they wear their hearts on their sleeves. Their daughters are, by contrast, complicated, aware of their manipulative abilities in relationships with people, and subtle in their behavior. They, more often than boys, develop an early and definitely stated taste in clothes. A boy may consent to wear whatever has been put out for him as long as he can also sport his Adidas running shoes and blue cap; a girl will wear only the underpants with the hearts, fall in love with a particular quilted bathrobe, and want only blue bows in her hair.

All these differences point to a single underlying one. In the year between their sexist second birthday party and their even more sexist third birthday party—Johnny invited mostly boys, Elizabeth mostly girls—children are developing an objective self-awareness toddlers lack. Like the baby's sense of self and the toddler's experience of gender, the two year old's dawning self-awareness is different in girls and boys.

It becomes somewhat difficult now to talk all in one breath about boys and girls as we did about babies and toddlers. But we can sketch in as background for both sexes their progress toward separation during the year commonly known as "the terrible twos."

Ambivalence—the terribleness of the two year old—is at its height. An embattled atmosphere thickens under the pressure of toilet training, and war rages over related issues of autonomy, from what to wear to how to eat. Toilet training epitomizes the issues surrounding autonomy. Crudely put, the question is: Whose body is this, anyway? Does it belong to the mother, who decides when and where urination and bowel movements are to take place, or does it belong to the child to manage in his own way? And are the child's body products, his beloved bowel movements in particular, his mother's possessions, to be wrested from him and disposed of as she wishes, or his own belongings, to withhold or grant as he sees fit? The extremes of the conflict represent a no-win situation, for on the one hand the route to a mother's love lies in compliance with her demands, and, on the other, separating from her demands noncompliance.

A happy resolution requires a measure of sophistication: the child must decide, as a free and independent person, to make his mother a gift of his compliance. This is usually achieved somewhere around three years old, perhaps earlier for girls, later for boys. The pact makes the mother a recipient, but not the possessor, of the child's bodily products. The child offers goods in exchange for the moral rewards of goodness. The deal is made between two separate people to the mutual satisfaction of both.

That the ambivalence subsides enough to allow a ceasefire in the war for independence at least for the present (the battle will erupt again with vigor during adolescence) is a general result of the two year old's increasing competence. He now becomes able to build with blocks, to scribble with crayons, to throw and catch a ball. The more he can do, the more enticing the world becomes, and the more real. Only a year before, a ball popped unexpectedly into view and disappeared as unreasonably; now it is the child's prized tool, giving him control over just such comings and goings. And that same ball has heaped up attributes that greatly add to its charms: it is now *big* and *red* and *mine*. More and more, reality seduces the child from his mother's side.

Language is another link providing the child with strong ties to reality, although it also serves to distinguish actual events from pretend. The two year old can call a piece of toast "toast" and eat it up, but he can also, knowing better, call it "car" and drive it across the breakfast table. So with maturity the child becomes both better connected to the real world and less pushed around by it. There is a greater area of experience in which his mother's assumed omnipotence is not felt or in which the child no longer needs to share her powers. There is less to feel ambivalent about, and gradually two year olds become capable of a more mature, give-and-take relationship with their mothers.

All these experiences affect the child's picture of himself, which during the year shifts from vulnerable subjectivity to a more stable objective image that can be checked and tested in reality and manipulated in fantasy. Since boys' and girls' play fantasy appears different by their entry into nursery school—Edward's prowling simpler than Martha's plots—the quality of their self-awareness can be expected to differ too.

At the beginning of their third year, children show that their sense of self is still subjective by the way in which they play hide-and-seek. When they are two, they hide in such a way that they can't see the person who is to find them and assume that person can't see them either. When they are immediately spotted, they are surprised and indignant. They can't imagine seeing from any viewpoint other than their own. By the time they are three, their game has improved. While they are still remarkably easy to find (they giggle loudly), they have come to appreciate the viewpoints of others and therefore hide themselves passably well. Now they know themselves from the outside as well as the inside.

The development of self-awareness between two and three can be traced by observing how the child's references to himself change. Jean-Fabien Zazzo's father kept extensive notes on how his son referred to himself during this year. Jean-Fabien first identified his own image in the mirror at the age of two years, three months.[1] He hesitated, uncertain, then proclaimed, "Dadin!", his name for himself. His father felt this first hesitant identification was more in the nature of "Look! Another Dadin!"

Like other children his age, Jean-Fabien did not use the pronoun "I" freely to form novel phrases but could use it in learned combinations in which "I" was embedded in the verb, as in "I'wanna" or "I'dunno." When referring to himself in novel phrases, he used his name, as in "Dadin go bye-bye." "Me" is often used at this age as an alternative name, as in "Me go bye-bye."

Five months later Jean-Fabien remarked for the first time of his mirror image, "That's me," and touched his finger to his chest. At about the same period, he began to use the pronoun "I" inventively for statements other than those he had memorized, though he still lapsed into earlier forms. For a while, correct pronoun usage is subject to such lapses and reversals. The child frustrates himself and everyone else by sometimes referring to himself as "you," as others do, which results in such confusing conversations as:

> "You want a cookie."
> "Do you mean *you* want a cookie?"
> "YOU want a cookie!"

Jean-Fabien, on a timetable that is probably about average, achieved consistently correct pronoun usage before his third birthday.

The grammatical feat is not simply one of building vocabulary but is a conceptual stunt comparable to leaping outside one's skin. The child must realize that all of the people that he calls "you" are "I" to themselves and that although he is "I" to himself, he is a "you" to everyone else. Mirrors and snapshots help the child to see himself as an object in a world of objects, a "double" of himself that can be seen as though from someone else's perspective; but the process occurs in mental imagery even without the help of external images. This sustaining self-awareness helps a child through threatening events. Ginny was able to survive shampoos with the help of a hand mirror and the various "horns" and "curls" her mother shaped in her sudsy hair. Self-awareness also helps a child manipulate others. Rafael practiced a pathetic facial expression in front of the mirror, mock-crying while peeking through his fingers to gauge the effect. Almost all children now begin to ornament themselves with makeup, jewelry, and fantastical costuming to augment themselves in their own and others' eyes.

The same process can be followed by noticing how the child represents himself in play. When a young toddler longs for babyhood, she may actually regress, as Donna did, by clinging to her mother or going back to a bottle she had earlier given up. She can only be babyish by becoming a baby. In time, she becomes able to pretend she is babyish, often with the help of a toy like a baby carriage or a doll's bed. At this point we can see some sense of self and other, as well as a distinguishing between reality and pretense, for the child is able to pretend both herself as a baby by mock-crying and herself as parent by remarking, in a different voice, "Here comes your bottle." But she must still be the subject of her own representation; the pretense occurs within her own body, which she has placed in the baby carriage.

Only when the child's self-image becomes objective, viewable from outside as well as inside, can she begin to represent herself externally in the form, for instance, of a doll or a stuffed animal—Donna caring for her babies. Representational play roughly coincides with the correct and consistent use of "I" and with self-assured identification of the child in mirrors and pictures during the latter part of the third year.

While the timetable for developing an objective sense of self seems to be about the same for girls and boys, girls may have both a greater impetus to achieve it and a particular flair for doing so. The impetus is their own untenable position during this year. Of course, both sexes are becoming more independent every day as they learn how to wash their hands, stir chocolate syrup into the milk, and zipper up their jackets. But girls do not experience these events in the same way as boys, nor do their mothers. Take an event as simple as a child learning to pour juice. The boy brushes his mother aside as if to say, "Look! I can do this without you." The girl turns to her mother as if to say, "Look! I can do this just like you." The event is identical, yet boys tend to see it as emphasizing their separateness, whereas girls tend to see it as emphasizing their similarity. The mother perceives the event in different ways, too. The more her son can do, the further apart their worlds grow. The more her daughter can do, the greater is their shared world.

Representational play offers the little girl a way out of this deadlock. As self-awareness grows and she can begin to represent herself and her parents outside her own body, she can create a new kind of distance between them. Over here is the baby, and over here the mother. Without actually moving off and without actually becoming different, she finds a pretend way to explore both her own and her mother's individuality.

Usually the character that stands for the child is like the little girl who had a little curl: either she is very, very good, or she is horrid. So is the character that stands for the mother. This is not just for the sake of drama; it is a way both male and female toddlers preserve a modicum of self-esteem despite scoldings, and also continue to love a mother who is so heartless as to leave them with a babysitter. They split apart the good from the bad in their mental imagery. The good mother is the one a toddler cries for when she walks out the door; the bad mother is the one he hits when she returns. Toddlers split their own self-image, too. This is most easily seen in those children who have an imaginary friend. The child, good boy that he is, could not possibly have spilled the milk. "Peter" did it.

Girls, with their greater ambivalence and lesser self-esteem after their discovery of the sexual difference, may require splitting a little more than boys do. At any rate, they appear in their third year to work harder at its resolution. Representational play may come to the fore earlier, become quite elaborate, and constitute the major play activity. Scoldings and weepings, aggressions and apologies are fired back and forth between the cats and dogs, babies and grownups of a girl's imagination. Goodness and badness are allowed to come together in the outside world, where their touching can't injure her. Here, in fantasy, is a kind of distance the girl can handle, and her pleasure in discovering it seems inexhaustible.

As before, parents are directed to participate in these new games, and mothers in particular may find they are spending much of their time gobbling up deliciously invisible cookies or berating naughty monkeys. As these games are safely played out through dolls, stuffed animals, and obedient parents, children become able to integrate goodness with badness first in their outer representations, and then in their inner ones as well. We can actually see it happening. Should a mother make an awful face, say "Yuck!" and spit the imaginary cookie out, her daughter is not alarmed. She may, in fact, feel so amused that she calls for endless repeat performances. This bad mother is a warmhearted partner; it is also all right for this good girl to serve worms in place of cookies.

The flair girls have for representational play may be related to their rather subdued mood at this time. While boys have been so forthrightly enacting their masculinity with roaring leaps and careening cars, thrusting themselves upon the world in optimistic denial, girls have coped with their awareness of the sexual difference in more contemplative ways. Also, the girl's gift for language comes in handy at this point, for it is largely through spoken negotiations that the characters come to terms with one another. (Mothers are shocked to hear their very words repeated, often in a way that gives them, too, perspective on how the other party in their relationship views their actions.)

The result of representational play for both boys and girls is that the child becomes a whole self in his mental imagery as well as in his play, and so does his mother.

By the age of three, most children are able to hold on to their sustaining bond with their mother whether she is in a good mood or a grumpy one, available or busy, at their side or out to dinner. She is a whole person, objective and separate, whose image burns with a steady flame in spite of the winds of circumstance. Our culture recognizes three years old as a graduation of sorts, for that is the age when we expect that our girls and boys will be able to leave their mothers for short periods and go to nursery school. Families seem to recognize their child's newly integrated view of himself, too. This is the time when endearments that seem to stand for both the child's charms and his mischief—Monkey, Imp, Bug—pop into family use.

With objectivity comes true separation, and now the little girl can begin in earnest the identification with her mother that will resolve her difficulties. Her interest in high heels, pink soap, Betsy Wetsy, and muffin mix picks up even though she may at the same time pursue tomboyish ways. Having given herself better distance through her own fantasy play, and girded now with an image of herself and her mother as two separate, whole individuals, each with a life of her own, most girls find it increasingly easy to choose those ways in which they wish to be similar to their mothers without at the same time merging with her. Yet the progress we have followed toward a resolution of separation issues, first by boys and then by girls, does not culminate in a definite end point at which we can say, "Aha! They have done it!" Most boys and girls enter nursery school with a separation sufficient for them to function as individuals, but functional autonomy remains relative.

For all of us, all through our lives, our autonomy wavers somewhere in between the poles of complete merging or complete independence, and our relative freedom is forever affected by our individual gifts, by the accidents of our personal biography, and by the many pressures circumstances continually exert on us. The separation issue is replayed, sometimes violently, during adolescence, and often again in middle age. Teen-aged girls are remarkably ambivalent with their mothers; middle-aged women unusually concerned to "find" themselves. The feminist movement has spotlighted women's struggle to define themselves without reference to their parents, husbands, and children, and the very bitterness of this uphill battle indicates how deep the problem lies. Separation continues as a particular issue of feminine identity for most of a woman's life cycle. Girls just do not come apart from their mothers in the same way as boys.

In spite of the earlier onset and greater intensity and complexity of a girl's representational play, the quality of her self-awareness is distinctively feminine. Girls turn out "gooder." Indeed, goodness becomes a central focus of feminine gender identity. Why should girls, who have been more critical, demanding, and impossible to please, now present themselves as the nicer of the two sexes?

Donna's very difficult struggle to overcome her anatomical "defect" can give us one clue. She, who at two and a half tried "osmosis" as a way to get what she coveted from males, continued to hope. She learned from an older brother and from her little boyfriend—and invented on her own—all sorts of body movements she called "tricks" (twisting her arms together or looping her back), and these she enjoyed performing for onlookers. She was wonderfully pleased with her abilities; her body was so fine, it could even do tricks. She had a baby doll whom she denied was either a girl or a boy, but only a baby, as though it were neuter and might still grow up to be either sex. One day when Donna had performed one of her tricks, she sobered and, looking down at her arm, called it a "baby arm." When she was feeling low, she called herself a baby. Only when Donna was feeling exceptionally good about herself could she call herself a girl.

Donna and other little girls of this age may commonly detect a real impatience on their mother's part. After all, they have been behaving rather badly. Unfortunately, a two year old can't see that it is her own clinging and coercing for the past several months, rather than her "defect," which displeases her mother. Armed with the strengths of objectivity, yet done in by its pitfalls, it seems reasonable that both she and her mother recognize her for what she is: damaged goods.

This is an interpretation most feminists would not agree with. They argue that the viewpoint is Freudian and that Freud was sexist. Freud was indeed sexist and also admitted he was mystified about little girls. But because his theories of female development do not square with more thorough observations, psychoanalysts have long since abandoned most of Freud's notions—except the girl's longing for a penis. On the subject of penis envy, the feminist psychoanalyst Karen Horney and others who followed her felt that girls understood the penis as a symbol for male power and privilege. They covet what goes with having a penis and not the organ itself.

The feminist movement in general has taken a somewhat more direct view. If girls think of themselves as damaged goods, that idea must have been taught to them—by fathers and brothers who put them down, by families and a society that make it quite clear that boys are better and back up that judgment by giving boys more freedom. But Horney's specific and other feminists' general arguments are hard to support. Since penis envy typically occurs abruptly when the child isn't even two years old, so sophisticated a use of symbol seems a rather tortured way of explaining it. After all, girls are explicit: they ask for a penis, not a privilege, and there seems no reason not to believe them. As for the more general assumption that girls are disparaged by their families and culture in their tenderest years, there is just no evidence to support it. Most parents are delighted to have a daughter, and fathers are often downright foolish over their little girls—who hasn't seen that and laughed about it? It's true that at a later age, though not in toddlerhood, boys put girls down, but girls usually manage to get back at them. The henpecked husband is as vivid an image in our culture as the downtrodden wife. And these little girls, only two years old, haven't read about how Little Red Riding Hood needed a man to rescue her or watched *The Stepford Wives*. Their own families, as we have pointed out, may be models of nonsexism.

And still, in every careful clinical study and in the observations we parents, too, can make, little girls this age seem to think they are not quite good enough.

One way for girls to fight back is to become more perfect—to stay within the lines and cut a neat edge—and this effort, bolstered by the girl's possible tendency toward deft movements, verbal precocity, and a gentle temperament, is what gives the three-year-old schoolgirl that first blush of "goodness." Mothers, caught unaware, may be as surprised to note how productive their daughters are in school as they are to see them burst into tears over a remark about dripped paint. Their little girl has become raw to criticism, a sponge to praise. Female vanity begins early.

We notice other differences, too. Johnny, while visiting his grandparents, was utterly charming, eminently verbal, and most interested in whatever was drawn to his attention. While his grandparents gardened, he asked for many rides in the wheelbarrow, hid behind bushes and called for them to find him, then turned his hands to a Have-a-Heart trap with which he hoped to catch a rabbit. His cousin Elizabeth fit more smoothly into her grandparent's activities. She rode in the wheelbarrow during Grandpa's trips to and from the toolshed and compost heap. While Grandma pruned dead flower heads, Elizabeth gathered a bouquet. When they sat down to rest, she hauled over a chair and chatted with them. While she was neither more nor less active and interested than Johnny, her play less often interrupted the flow of others' activities and more often complemented her grandparents' pace and mood.

This girlish behavior is more than a matter of rising above adversity by being good. It is a reflection of a girl's distinctive brand of self-awareness. Her sense of her own individual self seems connected from moment to moment with the views of others, as though that whole fabric of glances, smiles, and conversation is used now to keep her informed of who she is in relation to those around her. That girls now seem more aware of others' viewpoints may be in part because they come by them more easily. The very closeness with their mother from which girls suffer may give them a shortcut into her point of view. There is still an enormous gain in perspective, but from the beginning that perspective has an empathic quality, so that Martha, Lisa, and Jane not only seem on the lookout for their teacher's response to them but appear to experience those responses more vividly than boys.

One result is that girls may now strike us as more sensitive. They may already cry easily during sad movies and stories, and their tears feel good; the effect of the same movies and stories on boys is less extreme. Perhaps, from the boys' more distant vantage point, the feelings of others are less invasive. They perceive the emotions but don't actually feel them inside, and if those feelings should invade them and make them cry, they are usually upset. Boys can be very sympathetic, but empathy—feeling someone else's feelings as though they were your own—does not come easily to them. Feeling someone else's feelings comes too close to disrupting their sense of self, whereas it is very much a part of a girl's self and is often received with pleasure.

This sexual difference, although it is merely a sharpening of differences in an infant's closer or more distant sense of self and a toddler's similar or contrasting experience of gender, begins to fit better our understanding of masculinity and femininity. Women are easily moved by others' inner lives; men are less so. The gap, narrow now, is stretched dramatically by the repercussions of the three year old's self-awareness.

We will have to step back still further from the child now to look at a greater chunk of time, the years between his entry to preschool and "graduation" to elementary school at the age of six. This perspective will allow us to view a whole landscape that has as its foreground separation and at its horizon heterosexuality. Mother and child, the focus of our view thus far, are now joined by the father, who continues his role as the important "other person" in ways that increasingly place him in the middle of the picture. The father becomes the fulcrum for the further development of boys and girls during this period, although in ways that differ for sons and daughters. Just as the girl begins to find a more fruitful avenue to pursue, the boy's temporary resolution of his problems begins to fail him. His wonderful identification with his father, which, in its masculine bluster, was to charm his mother utterly, contains a hidden and dangerous trap. That trap only appears as he, like the girl, builds an objective sense of self.

During the preschool years self-awareness causes both boys and girls to become increasingly concerned with how they appear to themselves and others. For example, they protect their self-image by establishing their own taste in clothing and enhance it with costumes—just look at a boy exaggerating his masculinity by topping off his outfit with a cowboy hat. Their objective sense of themselves is not very secure, however. A three year old can terrorize himself by trying on a Halloween mask. The mask transforms him into a stranger; he had lost himself. Children's often tearful—and sometimes panic-stricken—reaction to a haircut is similar. Not only do they fear that the barber might wield his sharp scissors carelessly or with malice, they dread the loss of their hair.

Fear of deformation and injury emerges in a context that lends passion to what might otherwise be mere concern. We have seen that when boys and girls discover that only some people have a penis, it occurs to them that a penis could perhaps be granted or denied, tacked on or taken off. At about the age of three, sexual sensations seem to intensify, drawing the child's attention more and more to his genitals at just the time his self-awareness blooms. The result is familiar to all parents. When a toddler scratches his knee, he is easily consoled by his mother's "kissing the hurt away." That will no longer do for the three year old. He requires such a plastering of bandages that his parents can barely keep pace with the demand. Often we can't even see the injury that has caused such alarm or can't convince the child to remove his bandage, even long after a minute mosquito bite has disappeared. A broken toy, which was only a frustration to the two year old, worries the three year old considerably. He can't believe his parents' deficiencies as repairmen; he pesters them relentlessly to fix the unfixable. Refusal to accept damage is so pervasive at this age that many children will not eat a broken cookie or wear a frayed sock.

The child's more highly developed sense of reality is not the help we might imagine. First, parts of objects really do break off—a thought that is hardly comforting when the child contemplates the meaning of a "broken leg." Second, feelings he has projected onto external objects through his new talents at self-representation have a way of coming back at him. The lion he made to roar out his anger during the day snaps angrily at him in dreams during the night. Just as the child now can praise himself by internalizing the praise of others, so can he blame himself by incorporating the blame of others. His new openness gives birth to guilt.

Clinical work with children reveals that castration fear (and punishing bad dreams) are at their height just as the child is most passionately involved with the parent of opposite sex and just as that involvement is most obviously sexual.

For the boy, anxiety about potential injury automatically intensifies because of the masculine solution he has found for his separation problems. From his position of mutual masculinity with his father, he enters into an outright courtship of his mother as early as three years old. He shows signs of being quite in love. He runs little errands for her, brings her bunches of wilting dandelions, and offers to fix this and that around the house. But his courtliness is betrayed by frankly sexual advances. A son may startle his mother by using his tongue in a goodnight kiss, asking to stroke her breasts, even pushing his erect penis against her thigh. He wants to cuddle in bed with her and may begin to object when his father kisses her or dances with her. Ultimately, he proposes.

Needless to say, this tack leads the boy out of the frying pan into the fire. He can see quite clearly that his mother and father share a special and exclusive relationship. His father's patience, usually reliable, is tried when his son puts his hand down his mommy's dress or tries to oust Daddy from the marriage bed. Not only does reality suggest that such behaviors are not to his father's liking, but the boy himself begins to feel his father is his rival.

Jeff's rivalry with his father first appeared when the boy was only a little over two and a half. Jeff remarked that his penis was little while his father's penis was big, and later added that "the machine" would make his as big as Daddy's. If a little boy wants to have the exclusive relationship with his mother that his rival has—if he wants to possess her—Daddy will have to be gotten rid of. Three year olds have more than enough imagination to appreciate the dangers inherent in this scenario. A boy fully expects his father to resent being pushed aside as he is himself resentful of his father's privileges. Michael, who had shared with his father a particular pleasure in romping with the neighbor's large dog, began to think a dog might get mad at children and become afraid it would bite him. Though his own aggressively sexual feelings drive him onward, the three-year-old boy is unsure where they might lead. Daniel had a terrifying dream in which he was driving a car that went faster and faster, got out of control, and crashed.

These generalized fears that formerly benign figures will turn in anger or that doing manly things will lead to disaster only slightly disguise a very specific and very vivid fear of castration. When Jeff confronted his mother with his no-longer-to-be-denied knowledge of her penisless state, she explained that she had a vagina instead. Jeff replied, "Vagina hurt." The authors add that Jeff's mother, like most of the other mothers in their study, seemed to appreciate how central castration ideas are to their children and had therefore been scrupulous to avoid exposing Jeff to evidence of menstrual bleeding. Nevertheless, Jeff assumed injury.

Lurid fears are joined by a threat to the very mechanism by which the boy has arrived at his courtly and seductive masculinity: his loving identification with his father. Without his father's support, can he remain masculine? Can he really drive a car all by himself? And does he really want to get rid of this man whom he so admires and loves, and after whom he has so proudly fashioned himself? Unlike the girl, whose primary identity is feminine by definition, the boy has had to wrest his masculine identity from feminine union with his mother through difference and daring. Should he become "unmanned" in either a physical or an emotional sense, his very survival as a separate individual is at stake. In a psychological sense, this is a life-or-death situation. The choice the boy makes is without doubt the most momentous decision of his life.

The boy chooses to safeguard his masculinity by renouncing his mother as the specific object of his passion. His father can have her; he'll wait until he is grown up, when he looks forward to possessing some other woman (amusingly, at this point the boy may transparently choose a close substitute, such as a female cousin). Meanwhile, he is free to join his father in a "man's world" which, for some years to come, has little room in it for females of any age. Not that the boy has broken his bond with his mother. Quite the opposite, he has purified it of sexuality so that his love is defused, made safe, and thereby preserved. Boys continue throughout childhood to love and defend their mother, to admire her nurturing qualities while denying her sexual ones.

This momentous process unfolds gradually, usually from the time the boy is about three years old until he is about five, yet when the solution occurs to him it is carried out quite suddenly. One day the boy plants an exuberant kiss on his mother's mouth, the next day he is too old for kissing.

Just as the boy exits from his dangerous sexual entanglement with his mother, the girl enters the triangle the boy has been struggling with.

Sexuality presses at the three-year-old girl as it does at the boy; she, too, at first directs sexual feelings toward her mother. But her advances are not greeted with amused appreciation. They are probably not acknowledged as sexual at all, but rather as a continuation of the long-standing and intense physical intimacy infant girls and their mothers have shared. Their relationship remains sensual without becoming sexual. Further, the boy sees that his masculine form of sexuality interests his mother and is acceptable to her. The girl does not get that message. In fact, observing her mother's special relationship to her father and perhaps to the little girl's brothers, she feels defective not only in her anatomy but also in her ability to interest her mother sexually.

All the girl's real progress and all the support that parents and teachers can give her at this age do not seem able to redress her imagined wrongs, not just because she doesn't have what boys have, but because neither her route to her mother nor her freedom from her is so satisfying as a boy's. Her mother is just too mean—a criticism we are far more likely to hear from daughters than from sons.

Her father is a harbor to which the girl turns from the storm of resentment she still feels toward her mother. But during these years (three and four years old) when boys are quite passionate with their mothers, the girl's relationship with her father is not clearly sexual. Her father is not intended as the object of his daughter's seduction so much as he is to be her instrument for seducing her mother. Those special qualities about Daddy which so interest Mommy will rub off on her; she will learn from him the "tricks of the trade." So Daddy is a relief to his daughter, a help to her, a means to an end—but not yet the goal of her passion.

Compared to the sudden and vivid entry of the father into a boy's internal life, the girl lets her father in gradually and years later than is the case with boys. He is a satellite to the orbit she shares with Mother. Yet she finds his attentions supportive, flattering, and exciting. He treats her in a courtly manner, assumes her sexual interest (perhaps before it has appeared), and may treat his daughter to particularly arousing sensations as he jounces her on his knee or lets her ride horsey astride his shoulders. The appearance of intimacy, which was at first entered into for ulterior motives, gradually shifts to a real intimacy as her father actually does become her heterosexual choice. But this does not occur until the girl is nearly into kindergarten, nor does the girl's fall into love hit her so hard or plunge her so deep as the boy's.

The reason is that her father is *merely* her heterosexual choice. He can never become everything that a mother becomes for her son, for only a mother has both shared the bliss of unity and held out the promise of heterosexuality. Being "Daddy's girl" safeguards the little girl from her mother and gives her at last the full measure of distance she requires for her independence; but it does not ever completely distract her from her first love—Mommy.

There are other reasons, too, that a girl's turn to her father lacks total commitment. A father's love is rougher than a mother's, his arms more powerful, his skin scratchier, his voice more booming, and his sexuality, perhaps, more dangerous. Phallic phobias, such as the fear of snakes or of rodents, develop at this stage. From these fears of penetration and injury, alliance with her mother offers the girl protection. The girl vacillates. She goes to her father for freedom from her mother, to her mother for safety from her father. She is always looking over her shoulder; even as she nestles herself into her father's lap and folds herself luxuriously into his arms, she asks: What will Mommy think of this? Will she protect me? Will she abandon me? Will she harm me?

So, unlike the boy, the girl does not come to a clearcut resolution of the triangular affair she has gotten herself into. She doesn't want to and she doesn't need to. The same castration that the boy perceives as something that might happen in the future, the girl perceives as something that might have been done in the past and might be undone in the future. She does not feel pressed to give up that hope. Liz asked her father for boxing gloves for her birthday—she was to be six. Curious about what she might have in mind, he pressed her for more detail. It turned out Liz expected to grow up to be a man. When Liz's father told her that was not possible, Liz broke into bitter tears. Her father didn't give her the boxing gloves, and perhaps that was mean of him, but to withhold boxing gloves because they represent a futile hope does not put down a daughter's strength, agility, or quick eye on the ball. Many girls build a portion of self-esteem on their tomboyish abilities all through their school years, shedding that masculine support system only in adolescence and still retaining the skills. A girl's feminine identity is not threatened by a dose of masculinity as a boy's is by a dose of femininity, because the implications for loss of self are not the same. The words "sissy" and "tomboy" do not have equivalent pejorative value; the behaviors themselves are not signs of gender frailty.

Because the threat of castration is less urgent and the pull toward continued intimacy with their mother stronger, girls get to have their cake and eat it too. They choose to identify with their mother both for insurance and out of love, but do not renounce their father entirely nor suppress their sexual feelings completely. Girls play at being wifely to their father, cuddle in his lap, and enjoy his masculine attentions all through their school years and even into adulthood. Their interest in boys is never so muted as boys' interest in girls. As for their hope to gain, through intimacy with males, the penis whose lack precipitated their turn to their father, girls only partially give up hope. They accept their female state, but as a sort of bargain in which their fortitude will be rewarded in the future by possession of a man and of the baby he will give them.

Every move the girl makes improves her position somewhat without resolving her problems completely. The whole juggling act, with its triangularity, compromise, and ambiv-

alence, is itself the girl's solution. All through life, as we can
see most clearly in the feminist movement, females will expect to have their cake and eat it too. Moreover, the way
females develop gives them the flexibility to do so surprisingly
well.

We have looked at about the first six years of the process
whereby "neuter" infants become girls and boys. Beginning
with subtle biological influences—ones that are statistical only
and that do not predict the individual—and the very powerful
influences of the mother's relationship with her infant, we
saw that the baby at one year was probably already internally
formulated according to gender. The baby boy's relationship
with his mother led to a more sharp-edged and remote self-
image than the blurred and intimate self-image of the baby
girl. These differing selves are the core around which the
child constructs all the later understandings of himself that
we call gender identity. Even though the one year old is not
strikingly masculine or feminine, we can say that the child at
this age not only is his sex, as he has been all along, but is
experiencing his gender, too. Actual masculinity and femininity appear within a few more months as gender becomes an
issue in separation.

With the discovery of the anatomical difference between
boys and girls in the second year, children take another step:
they become aware of the basis for their gender. They know
themselves to be girls or boys, and they know what physically
makes them so. From this awareness, and as they continue
the arduous climb from union with their mother to clear separation from her, they become able to choose attributes of
their gender through purposeful identification. All the time
they are gradually being introduced to the heterosexual significance of their maleness or femaleness.

The further step we have traced in this chapter is crucial. It is beyond being one's gender, beyond being aware of
one's gender, even beyond choosing to incorporate aspects of
one's gender. This last step is accepting one's gender identity:

liking it, living it, taking on and taking in all the peculiar risks and pleasures being a male or a female implies. Yes, we must bear with our son's going "bang-bang" with popsicle sticks, with his underfoot collection of Hot Wheels and his overmuscled superheroes with their capes and boots and belts and X-ray vision. And yes, we must bear with our daughter's infuriating Barbie dolls. We must because we can't teach our children otherwise. These six years have involved far more than learning. Acceptance of gender and the ability to find pleasure in it are very real facts of life, fashioned by each individual out of fearsome conflict, intense desire, symbols, fantasies, skills, defenses, compromises, and fateful decisions. The child is left enormously more complicated than before and marvelously enriched. Most important, his or her falling in love and the decisions about how to manage love's dangers have added finishing touches to gender identity that give each sex the full flavor we recognize as masculine or feminine.

So great is the jeopardy in which boys imagine themselves that they slam the lid down hard. They "forget" the lovers they once were and turn to other interests, which they pursue with the same energy and passion once lavished on their mother. Four brothers, each observed at about four years old, typify ambition at this turning point in boys' lives. The oldest learned to repair electrical wiring, the next struggled to draw his home in cross section, the third sought answers to such elusive questions as "What is America?" and "What's outside the sky?", and the youngest tried to engage the other three in his plans to build a real car. We are reminded of Don Quixote, whose questing similarly drew energy from a (now) purified love.

Whatever biology encourages in the way of a "natural" masculine bent toward spatial, mechanical, and coordination skills easily finds expression within these distracting pursuits. Similarly, whatever human evolutionary history contributes to a male tendency to form cooperating hierarchial groups comes in handy now. Male alliance in general serves as a protection from the risk of getting too close to females, and

groups of school-age boys spend considerable time augment- ·
ing their masculinity by doing just those things women would
not like them to do—including holding spitting contests and
leaping out of trees. Specifically, the relationship between a
boy and his father is a prototype for male alliance. The boy
affiliates with his father not as his male equal, but as his
father's subordinate; the affiliation supports the father's position among other males—a phenomenon easy to see in the
goings-on at Little League—and also promises support to the
boy as he grows toward his adult position in the larger world.

Functioning in ordered, cooperating groups requires formal positions and regulations. Boys' aptitude for formulating
regulated hierarchies is so extreme that it's touching. Four
boys form a club. They first decide who will be what: President, Vice-President, Secretary, and Treasurer—that takes
care of all of them. Then the four officers decide the rules.
After that: nothing. (The joke of "M*A*S*H*" lay in the
absurdity of hierarchy and regulation that flies in the face of
function.)

As there is a prototype for male affiliation in the relationship between father and son, so there is a prototype for
regulation in the boy's own mental life. To affiliate with his
father and put the lid on his unacceptable desires, the boy
internalizes regulations he perceives as arising from his father. They may be casual remarks ("Come on, that's nothing
to cry over"), standards ("You must always play to win"), or
real threats ("If I ever catch you stealing, I'll beat the hell out
of you"). Whether his father's voice is gentle or overbearing,
that voice, taken inside, becomes to the boy the voice of conscience. The process begins in the period when the child first
identifies with his father; Jeff, we saw, tended to be more
obedient with his father than with his mother. To that friendly
basis for internalizing requests is added the father's real or
imagined threatening qualities. (Girls also may more readily
obey their father, but they don't have the boy's reason to fear
him.) An element of force enters; the boy hears requests as
though they were commands. Yet he mustn't remain too

afraid of his father, so he disconnects the speaker from what is spoken. Commands are disembodied and depersonalized, leaving them bare, abstract, powerful, and unchangeable. The abstract nature of rules and standards—rights, justice, law, honor—henceforth strike males as a fundamental attribute of morality.

Threat hangs over the boy's development in other ways. He will never be able completely to put aside the idea that emotional closeness and the temptations it arouses can do harm to his masculinity and therefore to his survival as an individual. He must keep his distance from girls, as can be seen by the way most boys avoid like the plague—or tease— their sisters and their sisters' friends. Boys exaggerate female weaknesses as though all females become hysterical at the sight of mice or could barely carry a bag of groceries into the house, while they simultaneously exaggerate male virtues, firmly insisting that only males build houses, boss families, or become president of the United States. A boy can honor women's domestic strengths and like them for their soft skin, good smell, and nurturing qualities as long as he can in the same breath disclaim his own interest in good eating habits and clean fingernails. Most boys spend much of their time as far from the house and as far from females as they can get.

Even exaggeration and avoidance are not enough. Because masculinity is not the underlying infantile sense of being that occurred in union with a female and was therefore feminine, but is instead a construction continually assaulted by the threat of merging, boys (and men) must constantly work to maintain the edifice. There is an air of vigilance in boys' behavior: they watch for signs of weakness, emotionalism or closeness that might indicate a flaw, or a crack though which masculinity might trickle out. These flaws and cracks they shore up and plaster over with actual proofs of strength if they can, with bravado if better materials are not available, or with defenses that provide at least an outer barricade from onslaught. Such masculine efforts are often remarkably successful and result in our traditional ideal of boyhood: innocent, adventurous, honorable, and no girls allowed.

All these developments the little girl, in her complicated but relatively unthreatened position, has less urgent need of. She does not constrain herself so severely and remains open in many ways not available to boys. Her energies can stay bound up in relationships with people, including her father, and she does not have to turn so drastically toward mastery in the external world of objects. Mastery itself can be used to participate in relationships, rather than to compete in a hierarchy or to bolster frailty. Girls master the intricacies of rope jumping and jacks so they can play with other girls, and even them they are proud to be the best, they don't feel that earns them the right to lord it over their friends. They master schoolwork in a context of approval from parents and teachers, without much competition with one another and without feeling weakened by compliance.

Although girls identify with their mother (and also don't identify with aspects of her they don't like), we cannot say that they affiliate with their mother. Beneath feminine identification lies female identity, a sameness and union that is egalitarian by nature. Groups of girls tend to be egalitarian, and while there is much caprice in female friendships, so that Rachel is out of the group this week, there is also great intimacy, so that she is likely to be back in the moment there is a new secret to share. A group of girls seems to be an end in itself. Girls' groups rarely plan projects in which each member has a specific contribution, but instead gather for an activity such as playing Monopoly or dressing dolls with intimacy and friendship as the purpose. When trouble arises within the group, it is usually solved by dispersing rather than by recourse to abstract concepts of justice or even by renegotiating the rules.

When girls do negotiate, their basis tends to be more subjective than boys'. Girls have not had to disembody parental admonitions so completely because the admonitions have not carried so dire a threat. The voice of conscience is more human, and more humane. In an unpublished recent study, college-age men and women were asked their stand on the issue of abortion and were also probed for the basis of their opinion. Although either sex was as likely to be for or against abortion, men supported their stand with abstract principles concerning human rights; women supported their stand in terms of human needs and obligations. Moral standards by which both sexes are guided are often identical, but the route by which they have been arrived at is different, more personal and probably more flexible for females, more abstract and probably more rigid for males.

Girls' feminine identity is not precarious as is boys' masculine identity. Girls are not devastated by being seen whittling as a boy might be devastated by being discovered knitting—if any boy would try knitting. Femininity, inherent in infancy and continuous with later gender identity, can afford openness without endangering integrity. It's an adage in advertising that you can sell to both boys and girls by emphasizing the masculine aspects of a toy, game, or breakfast cereal, but you can't sell to boys if you emphasize feminine aspects of any product. Both sexes want Wheaties; only girls want Holly Hobbie muffin mix.

By the age of six, boys' and girls' versions of life's unfolding story differ in astonishing ways. They tell different stories of where babies come from. Although we tell boys and girls the same facts of life (or even if we tell them no facts at all), kindergarten boys theorize that something external, usually food, has to go into a woman to make a baby in her belly. Girls the same age theorize that the baby is there all the time, waiting to grow. Of course, both are right, yet both mysteriously seem to slant the facts of life to their own point of view, the male providing the external agent of fertilization, the female having the potential baby inside her all the time.

Phebe Cramer, a psychologist at Williams College, expanding on investigations originally undertaken by Erik Erikson over forty years ago, explored these differing versions of life through children's imaginative play.[2] She asked boys and girls to create an exciting scene using whatever they wished from an array of blocks and miniature furniture, people, animals, and vehicles. Younger boys, four, five, and six years old, used the blocks frequently and almost always for outdoor scenes of roads and tunnels. These scenes were filled with activity: cars rushed along, policemen tried to keep things under control, yet there were fights, shootings, chases, and crashes. Girls of the same ages rarely used blocks or vehicles at all. They created indoor scenes, using furniture and people, usually family members, and occasionally animals, usually domestic animals. The figures were involved in peaceful pursuits or were simply sitting, napping, or watching television. When asked what it was that was exciting in such a scene or what happened, girls were often unable to say. Not one of the forty-five girls in the study built a roadway, and only one set up a scene of danger and violence. Cramer calls the female theme at this age "goodness indoors," which she contrasts with the male theme of "caution outdoors."

At the same ages, children's spontaneous drawings differ in a similar way. Boys' drawings in cultures as disparate as American and Bali are loaded with vehicles: cars, trucks, airplanes, rockets. Girls seldom include vehicles in their drawings and when they do, they are not central. Girls frequently draw pictures of flowers and use flowers to decorate many kinds of pictures. The phallic significance of vehicles is obvious, and we have seen that their use in play comes to the fore just as the boy becomes entranced with his penis. That the flower has a genital significance to the girl is harder to see but becomes evident in Cramer's work with older children.

As boys and girls approach puberty, their dramatic productions begin to take on a more sexual character. By ten and eleven years old, girls increasingly use blocks to enclose the interior scene they create. Sometimes these rooms have no entrances: there is no way in. But often there is an entrance and, like a flower, it is ornamented and elaborate—a fancy way in. Again, as with the younger girls, everybody is in repose, everybody is being good. Now, however, comes the action: a dog wakes up, a burglar sneaks in, a crocodile crashes through, and these figures cause a great ruckus inside.

At ten and eleven, the horizontal roads typical of younger boys give way to emphatically tall buildings. The buildings are often surmounted with turrets or ornamented with projections. Nothing happens inside these structures (often they have no interior space) and there are almost never ornamented entrances. But plenty happens outside. Planes zoom in and crash against the building or nose-dive to the ground. People clamber up the side of the tower, reach the peak, plummet down. Often the tower topples too.

The stories boys this age tell end with a topple too. At first things go well, there are heroic feats of daring and all sorts of obstacles are overcome—until the plane crashes. Girls have a different view. Everything is just awful at first. Everybody is poor, nothing works out, no amount of effort is rewarded. Then, with an almost crazy twist, virtue pays off: The heroine gets married, has babies, and lives happily ever after.

The masculine pattern is a series of satisfactions followed by disappointment. The feminine pattern is a series of disappointments followed by satisfaction. The difference is not to be found so much in the events themselves as in the sequence in which the events occur. The boy's story, like his tower, is a rise and fall. The girl's story, like what happens in her house, ends with the rise. Both versions reveal a fundamental stance from which boys and girls view themselves within the stream of life. We just can't avoid seeing that even though boys and girls live in the same world, they do not, beginning in infancy and more profoundly and emphatically as they advance through childhood, experience the world the same way.

Can nonsexist parenting reverse the tide? Certainly it can't by the schemes feminists have so far put forward. Nonsexist parents could—in fact they do—reverse their own roles, so that their children can plainly see that women can be brain surgeons and men can bathe babies. But sons and daughters alike perceive Mommy as a conglomeration of soft skin, milky smell, sweet voice, and soothing style. Babies know from nothing about brain surgeons. Parents can deprive a boy of guns, but not of his index finger and the words "bang-bang," or of the layers of meaning guns and bangs and fingers have to boys. Parents can teach a girl to go "bang-bang" too, but there is no glue to make the lesson stick. Nonsexists could wipe out all our toy stores, television shows, picture books, and Little Leagues to no avail. As far as we can tell, girls become girls and boys become boys without them.

What is so fascinating about becoming girls and boys during these early years is the wonderful convergence of so many pressures that arise from so many sources toward a culmination in gender identity. Befogging issues of nature versus nurture vanish, and we can clearly see that every influence augments all the others, so that we cannot analyze out one factor without appreciating the total configuration. The slightest difference in skin sensitivity or vocalization frequency of girl and boy infants assumes importance as we realize the exquisiteness of maternal response to such tiny clues. Those responses in turn become more dramatic to our eyes as we see how the baby must use them as he continually constructs his image and reconstructs his relationships with his parents. The pressures of maturation and the abilities maturation implies—intellectual skills such as remembering, representing, and symbolizing, physical ones such as manipulation and locomotion—feed into the differing experiences that will shape a child's gender identity. Parents' stereotyped responses, so hard to evaluate at first, make sense as children themselves demand recognition of their maleness or femaleness, and then make sense again as the *real* boy's and girl's actions—he actually does play ball, she really does play house—meet with their parents' approval. And the surrounding culture, too, as it mirrors back to the child images that, as if by coincidence, reflect the ways he has pictured things anyway, augments the meaning of gender and contributes distinctive details so that eventually even the pink booties take their place among the panoply of experiences through which a child becomes a girl or boy. All of these influences coming together and leading to the emergence of masculinity and femininity are the program by which babies become girls and boys.

7

CONFUSION

The powerful program of physical, psychological, and social influences seems so precise that it is easy to lose sight of how easily the process of achieving a gender identity might go awry. What if a baby boy behaves more like a baby girl? What if a mother fails to appreciate his growing independence or his need for a good dose of masculinity? What if there is no father at home, or the mother must be away for long periods, or the child suffers an injury just as he discovers the sexual difference? And what if the culture disdains the difference between girls and boys, attempts to undo it or reverse it?

The superficial answer to all these questions is that that is what makes the world such an interesting place. There is, of course, no such thing as a typical male or a typical female, but only endless variations that include every possibility from a "feminine" man to a "masculine" woman, all nevertheless "free to be, you and me." Were this actually the case, the problem would be a purely social one: How to get society to fully accept this broad range of behavior, regardless of sex.

But this breezy answer assumes that variation never results from an underlying confusion over gender identity or that, if there is confusion, it is enriching and pleasurable for the person who experiences it. Unhappily, there is evidence that "freedom" from a solid and assured gender identity underlies at least the extremes of variation, and that it is often felt as pain and perceived as injury to the child who suffers it. The path along which effeminate boys and masculine girls have come is often a bruising one. Their futures may well be homosexuality.

Parents of children whose behavior is inappropriate for their sex often tell a "from the beginning" sort of story. Richard Green, a professor at the State University of New York at Stony Brook, has reported the case of Toni, whose parents became alarmed at her masculinity by school age. Her parents claimed that Toni was, from infancy, quite different from her typically feminine sisters. [1] "It was since she was born that she has been this way," her father said. "From a tiny baby, she was never cuddly, where you could hold her. You would hold her a while, then she would become squirmish and active." His wife agreed. Speaking of toddlerhood, she recalled that Toni "would actually push you away. If you held her on your lap, she would push her arms to get down and go get a toy to play with." The mother couldn't find this little girl appealing. The father played baseball with her because "it seemed to come natural."

In contrast, mothers of effeminate boys frequently recall that this particular son was an exceptionally cuddly baby. One mother remarked that her son "had the features of a girl. He loved to be held. He was always smiling. Gee, most of the time I would spend holding him." Fathers remember these sons as unresponsive to their approaches and unlikable.

These common reports suggest that the infant whose behavior is unusual compared to traditional expectations for his or her sex may be predisposed to weak gender identity as well. Are there biological influences at work here? The question is important because biology has often been used to explain—or explain away—homosexuality.

Recently, researchers have looked to hormones as a key to atypical gender identity.[2] Attempts to link hormonal balance in puberty or adulthood to homosexuality proved fruitless. The hormonal balance of homosexuals is quite ordinary, and people who do have an abnormal hormone balance don't become homosexual or experience a weak gender identity. Research into the effects of hormones during fetal life, however, has been more productive.

During the first weeks of life, male and female fetuses are virtually indistinguishable. The streaks of tissue that will become internal sex organs and external genitals are the same for both. At about the sixth week of gestation, however, a portion of this primitive tissue in a male fetus is instructed by its Y chromosome, which only males have, to begin its differentiation into male gonads, the testes. The hormones produced by the testes, particularly the androgen testosterone, then guide the continuing development of male genitals. Without the Y chromosome, ovaries develop instead of testes. And without the androgens that testes produce, the fetus will continue its development according to the female pattern regardless of its genetic sex.

These anatomical events, however dramatic, appear superficial compared to the profound effect hormones have on the fetus's developing brain. For example, the cyclic release of hormones typified in women by menstruation is extinguished in the male by androgens working on the neural pathways of the fetal brain. The proportion of androgens to estrogens also establishes the neural pathways that control activity level, energy expenditure patterns, exploratory behavior, and competitiveness. There is a hint from very recent work that testosterone, by inhibiting the growth of the left hemisphere of the brain during a portion of fetal life, allows the right hemisphere to develop more fully.[3] If this is so, it might explain why males are more frequently left-handed, have some difficulties in language (particularly reading and writing) and have a better grasp of spatial relations. The differences may reside in the relative complexity of neurological pathways in the two sides of the brain, each of which contributes to mental life in somewhat different ways.

The hormonal balance by which the fetal brain "decides" the fateful paths its neurons are to follow is a delicate thing, and the fetus's own production of androgens and estrogens does not have exclusive control over it, at least in animals. Experiments with laboratory animals have shown that stress on the mother during pregnancy or hormone-like drugs that she is given affect her litter's brain development and ultimately their behavior. Even the fetus's position in the uterus and how many males there are compared to females have measurable effects on later "masculine" and "feminine" behaviors. We don't know whether in humans, also, a mother's psychological state, the medications she is taking, or even multiple birth could affect how smiley or squirmy her newborn baby is. We do know that gross abnormality in the hormone balance—enough also to affect the anatomy of the sex organs—does affect temperament and thus the way the mother and baby respond to one another.

During the 1950s, a progestin drug was given to some women to prevent miscarriage. Although the hormone was considered an estrogen because of its effect on the mother, the chemical structure was similar enough to an androgen to masculinize a small number of the daughters born to women treated with it. In the disorder, female babies are born with masculinized external genitals, which may be as slight as an enlarged clitoris or as severe as a complete penis and (empty) scrotum. Internal sex organs are not affected.

Surgical correction was done shortly after birth, and these operations were very successful. The little girls could be expected to continue to develop as females, to menstruate, enjoy normal sexual activity, bear children, and nurse. As a group, however, they did not behave in typically girlish ways; nearly all of them were tomboys, and proud of it. They reported it, their parents and teachers agreed, and observations confirmed it. John Money of the Johns Hopkins Hospital studied these girls in detail, looking in particular at their choice of friends, clothing preferences, athletic skills and interests, behavior in childhood squabbles, and satisfaction with their gender. The results were clear: girls who had been masculinized during fetal life preferred to play with boys, preferred serviceable rather than dressy clothes, had a high degree of athletic skill, and particularly enjoyed competitive sports, with games such as baseball and football highest on their list. Careers interested them more than marriage and motherhood; at most they felt they might combine career and marriage, but few ever played with dolls and none wanted marriage exclusively. Like boys, they were markedly exploratory and active, preferring the outdoors to home and energetic to sedentary activities.

Some of Money's data are hard to explain. For example, quite a few of the girls played with trucks and guns even though they could not symbolize phallic activities from the sensations of their own surgically corrected genitals. Perhaps that thrusting urge is determined by neural mechanisms that are merely augmented in boys by actual experiences. Also, although the girls were competitive, they did not compete for a position in the male hierarchy. Money thought this might be because they saw competing with boys as unwise. They were, after all, girls, and would not have been accepted in boys' games had they crossed the line that separates the sexes. But another reason might be that these girls' fathers treated them like daughters, not like sons. Male-to-male relationships are forged in context of separation from the mother and alliance with the father. Greater levels of activity, athletic skill, and competitiveness only make it more likely that a boy will come upon this avenue of masculine development and mobilize his biological gifts toward that end. These girls may have been tomboys, but they were nevertheless their mothers' daughters.

And their gender identity was female. That is, all perceived themselves as females and none expressed a wish to become a boy. They were not, however, entirely pleased. Only 47 percent claimed to be completely satisfied to be female; 33 percent were not sure which was the better sex to be; and a startling 22 percent said they would have preferred to have been born boys.

Money's study was done when these girls were at school age. To learn about the girls' sexuality and sexual choice, a follow-up study was done on some of them after they had reached adolescence. Their ambivalence had not resulted in a higher than normal rate of homosexuality. But though heterosexual, their interest in boys was not marked, and their first love affair came considerably later than average. Menstruation was also late, even though their own hormone production had always been normal. Since boys generally experience puberty and fall in love about two years later than girls, perhaps the delay in menstruation and dating in these girls is due to something in their fetal development. Their "clocks" may have been set to male time.

A counterpart to the girl who is born masculinized is the boy who fails to masculinize because of insufficient androgens during fetal life. The condition is a rare one called androgen insensitivity. Hormone production is normal, but tissues throughout the body are unable to respond to androgens and so external female genitals develop. Corrective surgery to construct male organs is not satisfactory, nor would hormone treatment in adolescence succeed in giving these boys the voice, build, or beard of a young man. Generally, these children are raised as girls. The development of internal female organs has been inhibited by another hormone male fetuses produce, so they cannot look forward to pregnancy or menstruation; but the missing portion of the vagina can be constructed and their own or therapeutically administered estrogens during puberty assure a completely feminine body.

Genetic males with androgen insensitivity are not tomboys. Money, using the same measures he had used on the fetally masculinized group of girls and on a control of normal girls, found the androgen-insensitive group to be indistinguishable from the normal group. In striking contrast to the ambivalence that the masculinized girls felt about their gender, 90 percent of these girls reported themselves completely satisfied to be female. Like other girls their age, they daydreamed about marriage and babies, loved pretty clothes, jewelry, and perfume, and played almost exclusively with girls and with dolls.

The recollections of parents of effeminate boys and masculine girls are probably accurate: Their babies were not typical boys and girls from the beginning. Babies probably do come into the world predisposed to behave in ways that we perceive as masculine or feminine, and if these ways are not in keeping with their actual gender, these children have a tough row to hoe.

It would be a mistake, however, to view predisposition as predetermination. Between the time parents first greet their newborn baby and the time that baby has become a girl or a boy, a long story has unfolded. It is the whole plot of that story, not only its opening lines, that tells us how gender identity comes into being. The story for boys who become effeminate is quite different from the story for girls who become masculine, and the story for either is quite different from that of children who are typical of their sex.

To understand the full conspiracy of events behind a failure of masculinity, we will take a biographer's detailed approach. This particular story is a fascinating one; identical male twins (proved so by tissue-matching techniques), one of whom developed as an uneventfully masculine boy, the other one as a strikingly effeminate boy.[4] As in a Shakespearean drama, the story is presaged with the flavor of destiny. The father, the last male in his family to carry on its name, was very eager to have a boy. The mother wanted a girl. When twin boys were born, it seemed appropriate to both parents to name the firstborn after his father: Frank. Frank was the masculine twin. Here is the mother's description of the new babies, Frank and Paul:

Frank just took off like a little old man. He never looked like a baby. Never. Paul did. He looked the picture, with the rosy cheeks, round face, blue eyes, blond hair. . . . Paul was always the cuddlier of the two boys. You could hold him. You tried to hold Frank, and he would do everything but bite you.

Both the mother and father agreed in their descriptions of Frank, the masculine twin and his father's namesake. They recalled his looks at various times as "like a spider monkey," "like a drowned baby bird," and "very ugly." They were not the only ones to perceive the difference. Although the mother always dressed the two boys in identical clothing when she took them out in their stroller, it was not unusual for strangers to remark of the twins: "Oh, how nice! A boy and a girl!"

The parents were asked if they had noticed any difference in activity level during infancy. The mother recalled:

Up to four months there was nothing you could identify. After that I would say Frank over Paul. When they were still in the playpen, which puts them a little under a year, Frank reached over and bit Paul on the ear something fierce, and Paul didn't do anything. He just curled up.

Over the next two years, the parents did not notice any behavioral differences other than the temperamental ones that had appeared at playpen age. Certainly Paul was more gentle and more attractive than Frank, but this amount of variation between siblings—even twins—is not remarkable and does not preclude an unequivocally masculine identity for both. We can guess, though we cannot prove, that there was an important inner difference. Paul was held and cuddled more, whereas Frank kept himself at a distance even as an infant. Paul's sense of himself may well have been less separated from his mother; Frank's self was clearly rather distant from the start. As the twins entered the battlefield of separation toward the end of toddlerhood, they could not have been at an identical starting point. Paul was in some ways the girl his mother had hoped for; Frank certainly was not.

At this point in the story of a child's development, the father usually steps dramatically onto the stage almost as a deus ex machina, the hero who will resolve the predicament. But at this point in this story, Paul became seriously ill. His illness caused considerable pain and disability in one arm and meant hospital stays over the next two and a half years, from the time Paul was three to when he was about five and a half. His mother took him to the hospital and stayed there with him. While she was gone, the father stayed home to care for Frank, mostly whiling away the time with sports.

The entire family adapted to Paul's illness. Naturally, his mother became more protective of him and waited on him, but so did other members of the family. As the mother reported:

> Paul was always invited to be included with his brother, to participate, whether it was kite flying or basketball or baseball, but he didn't. . . . All the females in the family said, "You can't do that to him. That isn't his cup of tea."

Within a year, when Paul was four years old, both parents found it increasingly hard to ignore disturbing differences between the brothers: Paul now preferred playing with girls and dolls. The mother reported:

> His brother [Frank] was becoming very masculine at the time. Paul didn't want to participate in sports. He'd much rather clean house. I don't know whether it was a preference for me or for what I did, the fun of getting all dressed up or putting on make-up or doing dishes or grocery shopping.

By the time Paul was eight, he exhibited onerous signs of effeminacy. Like all such boys, he avoided any rough-and-tumble play (all homosexuals report avoiding physical fights in childhood, even if they become "fighters" as athletes or politicians in later life). He took female roles in dramatic play, was devoted to dolls, and, to his parents' distress, dressed in female clothing. The conspiracy of events was best summed up by his mother as she worried aloud that to Paul "it almost looks . . . that he [Frank] got Daddy's name because *he's the one that Daddy liked.*"

Much has been made of singular phenomena—the "smothering mother" or the abusive father—to explain the causes of homosexaulity. But here we have a story without a villain. This mother did not mean to keep her son so close to her; he appeared to require and welcome her closeness. This father did not mean to reject his son; the boy was removed from him and also rejected his advances. Accidents— Paul's adorable looks and warm cuddliness, his illness and real inability to participate in sports, even his birth order, which denied him his father's name—conspired to tip the balance from what might have made Paul a gentle boy to what made him an effeminate one.

We are left with the feeling that the cause is mere coincidence. A pretty, cuddly baby; a mother who responds to that baby with sufficient contact to hinder his separation from her; a further event (or fantasy) that leads the mother to protect the boy overmuch; the failure of the father, for whatever reason, to encourage masculinity, and perhaps a few more ingredients. A surprisingly pervasive finding is that many boys who become homosexual lacked male playmates during their earliest years. Most crucial, and most difficult to understand, the parents of effeminate boys do not discourage the earliest signs of feminine behavior. Some are indifferent. At first, most parents think that the boy is "cute" or "funny" when he prances about in his mother's evening slippers or artfully makes up his face. Not a few mothers, grandmothers, aunts, or sisters have aided and abetted the little boy—they have dressed him in female clothes before he had done so for himself.

When we look at the complicity of parents in the feminizing of their son, we must look deep into ourselves. If we are mothers, we have been little girls. We may have reason to wish to undo the difference between the sexes. The feminist quoted early in this book, musing on her son as he lay in his nightshirt drawing delicate pictures, was conscious of her desire to feminize him. Perhaps many mothers have such thoughts. If we are fathers, we have been little boys. That struggle, too, has been very great; the temptation to give it up is not beyond imagining. There may well be in all human beings a deep ambivalence about gender, and, as happens so early when the discovery of the sexual difference is first made, a wish to be the other sex, or both sexes.

The fantasy of being both sexes is aptly expressed by the male homosexual. He is like a woman—with a penis. The fantasy, however, is not a happy one; it is only the best he can do given the circumstances of his life.

These babies separate from their mothers in the same way as other boys, in keeping with their mothers' sense of difference from them. During toddlerhood, they like their penises and may show the beginnings of masculine interest in hoses, trucks, and guns, even though they may be, by nature, gentle boys. But when they try to resolve the issue of separation, to form the masculine type of bond with their mother, they are in trouble. For all the reasons apparent in Paul's story or similar circumstances in other boys' biographies, they can't mobilize their masculinity as they come to recognize their separation from their mothers. They can't use it to gain distance or independence, and they can't use it to woo their mothers either. The mother likes him girlish; the father doesn't help. For such boys, masculinity is an appendage.

Once a boy has achieved a masculine gender identity, however, he must cling to it, no matter how stacked the odds against him are and how heroic his effort will have to be. To give up masculinity is to lose more than a mere symbol: it is to lose his self. Preserving masculinity becomes a matter of survival to these boys.

Effeminate boys who become homosexual survive by creating a kind of joke. The joke is that they only *look* girlish. That is an acceptable wrapping. Beneath the wrapping is the punch: a potent male. In adult life, other men will be tricked by this joke into giving up what the boy's father failed to share, the masculinity the boy so longed to have from him. Women will be tricked, too (and mocked by the parody), for they have not quite succeeded in robbing the child of his maleness. Like all jokes, mastery comes by turning the tables: the victim becomes the perpetrator. The laugh that follows is one of both relief and revenge.

The dynamics by which a little boy does the best he can to be a boy even if that means masquerading as a girl or directing his sexuality toward other males are not comparable to the dynamics by which a little girl finds her way toward female homosexuality. Girls normally remain in an ambivalent attachment to their mother for years longer than boys do, try to win her in boyish as well as girlish ways, and seldom cap their effort with the finality typical of boys. We seem to understand this intuitively, for we do not fear tomboy behavior in girls as we fear effeminate behavior in boys and do not worry that it will end in homosexuality. Indeed, it rarely does. The foundation of feminine gender identity is laid deep in infancy. It need not be constructed from the ground up nor buttressed rigidly. Feminine identity relies instead on suppleness and can bend to considerable stress. The stress that femininity cannot take is that directed at its very foundation—the sense of sameness shared between mother and daughter.

A failure to feel safely unified with the mother is a condition of female homosexuality. Sometimes the failure can be traced in part to an actual rejection of the infant girl by her mother, but just as often the condition is circumstantial. The mother may be very ill during her daughter's infancy, or so depressed that she takes care of her baby in a perfunctory and detached way. At an earlier age than most, these girls may become unusually competent. They must do for themselves; they may also have to do for their mothers. Whether the mother is rejecting or simply helpless, identification with her is difficult. To identify with one's rejector is to reject oneself. To identify with helplessness is to remain helpless. Yet the girl's longing for her mother begs expression and demands satisfaction, if not in sameness with her, then in contrast to her. Most, perhaps all, little girls toy with a boy-style courtship of their mother. These little girls, however, become committed to it. They have no choice. Their femininity, already stressed at its foundation, lets them down; first, because it fails to bring them close to their mother; and second, because it fails to be of use in enlisting their father's aid.

As fathers of effeminate boys have been unable to support their son's masculinity, fathers of masculine girls have been unable to complement their daughter's femininity. Perhaps they have not been around enough to do so: they are in service stationed away from the family or are estranged from their wife. Just as likely, the father lives at home but feels beleaguered by women and awkward with them. Sometimes his discomfort takes a brutal turn, and his seductiveness with women is so indiscriminate and impersonal that even his own daughter cannot feel safe in his arms. But in the most extreme cases he appears—in a way—to be the ideal father. He becomes his daughter's ally in much the way most fathers become their son's ally.

A chumminess, a congeniality springs up between them, and they are very close. The closeness is, again, like that between a father and son in that the girl identifies with her father quite purposefully, stepping into his shoes and participating in his masculine activities easily and naturally as Toni's father described. Circumstances may contribute. The father may be substituting for his wife during her illness or absence at a point in development when young girls are, according to maturational requirements, searching for a loved person with whom to identify.

With the way to both identification with her mother and complementarity with her father blocked, the little girl is forced into masculinity. And masculinity turns out to be useful. If Father is not around, the girl can be her mother's little man. If her father is uncomfortable with daughters, she can be his boyish pal. And if he frightens her by being overly seductive, what better safeguard than to shed her femininity? In every case the little girl remains her mother's steadfast suitor.

There is no masculine counterpart to the word "effeminate." Femininity, because it is a primary state, cannot later be constructed; it can only be mimicked or parodied, as when an effeminate boy lisps, even though lisping is in no way typical of girls. Masculinity, while it may require experience of distance and difference, can be built even by a little girl, and when it is, it is not easily distinguishable from the genuine article. Unlike tomboys, whose boyishness does not strike us as incompatible with their femininity, very masculine girls are not girlish at all. They will not wear a dress under any circumstances. They know they cannot become boys, but that is what they wish to be. Effeminate boys do not wish to be girls.

Masculine girls do not give up heterosexuality so much as they fail to reach it; their goal remains their mother and does not become their father. Effeminate boys have reached heterosexuality only to retreat from its dangers; women remain the enemy. For the masculine girl, men are less despised than they are ignored, at least sexually. Nor does the girl's solution to her pressing problems contain the malicious wit of the boy's seemingly similar solution. There is no punch line, no phallus up the sleeve. Beneath the masquerade there is only a little girl hoping that she will be perfectly, completely loved if only she can be boy enough to suit. Looking at their earliest years, the effeminate boy's gender identity can be characterized as a threatened masculine identity; we can characterize the masculine girl's more accurately as a disappointed feminine identity.

The difference between female and male homosexual relationships in adulthood was captured unexpectedly in a series of interviews with lesbian mothers.[5] The interviews were conducted in order to learn more about children raised in lesbian families. A control group of mothers who chose to bring up their children in a single-parent home was also interviewed. Most of the mothers from both groups had either once been married to or lived with a man. They were asked about the quality of that relationship and the reasons for their eventual separation. The heterosexual mothers gave a variety of reasons for the failure of their relationship: abuse, desertion, unfaithfulness, alcoholism, sexual problems, the decline of love. Lesbian women were surprisingly uniform in their response: They maintained warm feelings for their former spouse or lover, and they claimed that their sexual lives had been satisfactory. The relationship had failed because they could not find in heterosexuality the intimacy they longed for. Intimacy, closeness, union of the intensity they craved could be found only with another woman.

By contrast, adult male homosexuality commonly precludes intimacy. Threat of union—and the loss of the very core of masculinity that implies—originally propelled the boy into homosexual fantasy. The continuing threat of union propels the man into the impermanence, hostility, and promiscuity that too often mar homosexual reality. Conversely, the more certain a man feels of his masculinity, the better able he is to endure intimacy, just as the more a woman feels her femininity is workable, the less constant and pressing is her need for intimacy.

The accounts cited here of how a boy or a girl comes to be homosexual are extremes in which the outward signs of markedly effeminate or masculine behavior were evident during childhood. Indeed, the biographical evidence for these cases is so detailed only because the children were referred for psychological treatment while the childhood events were fresh enough in the participants' minds to be reconstructed with a fair degree of accuracy. But there are children who grow up to resolve the struggles of their early years by homosexual commitment without signaling their confusion early on. To the world at large they are masculine enough or feminine enough to "pass." Much less is known about them. There may-be varying intensities of circumstances or temperament that would explain the greater subtlety of their behavior. The timing of crucial events as the program for heterosexuality unfolds may be even more important in affecting their eventual sexual preference.

Very masculine girls like Toni experience a failure of unity with their mothers that is quite severe and dates from infancy.Were that period to be "good enough"—even if it were not optimal—a little girl could find a reliable route to her mother's love through identification. She would appear unremarkably feminine. However, her turn to heterosexuality seems to have little to do with femininity per se. As the little girl attempts to mobilize her father's attentions in her push toward autonomy at about the age of four, she is at a particularly vulnerable juncture. If her father is overly frightening, if he rejects her, or if there is no father there at all (nor anyone to act as father), then the necessary pact between them cannot come about. In every case, she is thrown back upon her mother, her original—one might almost say primordial—love. All the urges for closeness and sexual union are in place, but without courtly seduction, complementary closeness, and a hint of future gratification, the shift to heterosexuality does not have sufficient promise.

In contrast, a boy always make it to heterosexuality in the sense that his love for his mother inevitably takes a sexual turn. His inability to continue in that direction is defensive, a matter of degree as well as a matter of timing. If Paul's illness had been less crippling, if it had occurred later, or if his father had been more an indoor tinkerer than an outdoor sportsman, he might have adopted a more masculine orientation. Given lesser intensity of circumstances or another year for development, he might at least have been able to cover his fears beneath a facade of masculinity, which, though thin, would have bolstered him somewhat and made him stand out less than the very effeminate boy he became.

Masculinity is vulnerable. Wrenched from an original feminine identity, it is preserved through rigid definitions and

This couple has given their school age son a thorough education in feminism, why there is a need for a women's movement, and how he can aid women's fight for equality and justice.

"We've explained to him how the bad men through the ages have hurt women, and at the same time hurt men by telling them what kind of men they should be. Our son knows he's in the vanguard of being a different kind of man. . . ."

Sometimes his resolve to be one of the vanguard, one of the "good men who help women," weakens and he is wracked with tears and sobs that he's afraid he won't be good enough. He fears the "bad men will get him."[6]

Carmichael then goes on to ask, "Is this pressure on a young boy too much? Are his parents doing him a disservice in asking him to be different?" She answers her own question by asserting that it is better than asking a child to live up to the standards of a John Wayne or a "super-jock." These parents are only asking their son "to decide for himself just what kind of man he is going to be, and to encourage him to measure himself against his own standards."

The little boy in the nightshirt described in the first chapter exemplifies the problem. His father, as it happens, was not living with him. His mother was wary of masculinity and grieved the potential loss of her son to its clutches. The problem is, she may not lose him. Femininity in a boy that age does not usually portend liberation. It portends femininity. When parental efforts are based on an underlying—even unconscious—disappointment in the sex a child is, trouble lies ahead. These two examples represent a plain failure to meet a child's need to like the sex he is, and to be sure that his parents like it too. But this is just what our little boys turn to their mothers and fathers for. They ask us to help them to be masculine.

Even when a boy is notably effeminate or a girl notably masculine, a diagnosis of future homosexuality is not always valid. Most of the children whose histories and characteristics are known in detail are not yet adolescents; their ultimate sexual choice is not known. Any presumptions are based on the fact that their stories very closely resemble those of adult homosexuals as they view their childhoods in retrospect. Masculine girls especially do not lend themselves to a prognosis. Tomboyism very frequently serves the childhood function of first wooing, and later establishing independence from the mother. During adolescence, boyish ways are traded in for the feminine insignia of heterosexuality, often quite dramatically over a brief period of time. Such girls may remain athletic, prefer serviceable clothes, and tenaciously pursue careers. They do not become mannish, and they do not become homosexual. Students of uncertain gender identity during childhood have suggested only one clue that might, if it eventually can be validated by long-term follow-up, point to later choice of sexual partner: childhood daydreams. One masculine boy who later became homosexual had a childhood fantasy of being overcome by male wrestlers. A feminine girl who later became homosexual daydreamed of being a knight on a white charger rescuing a beautiful maiden. Were childhood daydreams to prove precursors of adult erotic fantasies, there is still a problem: children do not ordinarily tell anybody their daydreams.

If they did, we would probably be forced to consider whether there is such an entity as homosexuality at all or, indeed, whether heterosexuality is its opposite. The either/or mentality we are accustomed to blinds us to the uncertainties of gender identity suffered not only by those who find relief in a homosexual way of life, but by many who achieve union with the opposite sex. Many transvestites, for example, are able to retain their heterosexuality exactly through the protective device of cross-dressing. Other "perversions," too, are erected to guard against dangers as they are perceived in the minds of very young and still quite helpless children. Heterosexuality itself never quite comes off untrammeled by protective fantasies or disguised longings which, though they are not shared with others during childhood and may not be admitted to waking thought when we become adults, nevertheless intrude into our dreams.

Childhood is innocent—not in the sense that it is without sexuality or malice, but in the sense that it is unsophisticated, a pitting of intense desires against limited knowledge and of vivid dangers against flimsy defenses. When she was three, Sally tried valiantly to grow a baby of her own by snitching the vitamins her pregnant mother was taking to "make the baby grow." When that strategy didn't work, Sally didn't come to the commonsense conclusion that she wasn't old enough but surmised that she had no "eggs." Never mind that other little girls weren't pregnant either—perhaps they hadn't discovered the secret way females go about growing a baby or didn't want one so badly or didn't feel that their mother, in her intense sharing of her pregnancy, had implicitly promised that Sally would have a baby, too. In fact, Sally's caring mother brought home from the hospital both her own real baby daughter and a baby doll for Sally. Disappointed and angry, Sally stopped playing with any dolls, stopped dressing up, and pretty much gave up on being a girl. When she became pregnant with her first child as a young woman, she was genuinely astonished, as though some miracle had happened.

Mark took his mother's frequent comment—"You should have been a girl" at face value. He became unable to look at himself in the mirror or to show a normal interest in clothing, as though his prettiness was a present danger; he might turn into a girl. Mark, too, was hampered throughout childhood and adolescence and only gradually became able to even shave in front of a mirror.

Of course, such fragments are not the whole picture puzzle, and in these cases the parents themselves rather fancied the daughter as a son, the son as a daughter. Children, for all their naïveté, are wonderful mind readers. The actual memories that surface only indicate the peg onto which they have hung an inarticulate understanding of their positions. That position is often an unhappy one. In adulthood Sally's and Mark's confusions were signaled by undue passivity, stridency, impotence, frigidity, and a host of other obstacles and discomforts that were very crippling. We all, as children, have only done the best we could. That best effort results in painful confusion far more often than is commonly believed.

Feminist ideology itself expresses a confusion over feminine gender identity. There are feminists who wish to undo the sexual difference, as though they had never recovered from their own early disappointment. Male children are okay if they come without water pistols; female children are better if they come with baseball bats. Mother—and motherhood—is disparaged; she is still to blame. This bitterness has in recent years lost many young women from the movement and slowed the effort toward some of feminism's most admirable goals. Betty Friedan, in her book *The Second Stage*, realizes and regrets the movement's anger and narrowness. She calls now for a new feminism that will acknowledge women's unique gifts and honor their desire to be wives and mothers. She sees the need to attract men's support, too. We can understand why male membership in feminist warfare has been merely lukewarm. This has not seemed to be their problem. And they have problems of their own.

It's hard to be masculine, harder than it is to be feminine. As many men must suffer from a secret wish to surrender as women suffer from their more open wish to vanquish. Our culture and all cultures are rife with henpecked husbands, Peter Pans who never grow up enough to declare their sex, and Amazons who might be women but seem like men. Ambivalence about gender is universal. We may think it female to be passive, to surrender; we may think it male to tough it out and jam it through. At one time or another, however, most of us want to do both.

Thus we are faced with the possibility that there may be no objective standard by which we can say what is a gender disorder and what is not, for to do so we would have to say where on the scale of relative ambivalence normal behavior ends and deviant behavior begins. But that's a question for professionals. As parents, we can be satisfied with a subjective standard. Every child tries very hard to be a boy or a girl. Painful confusion results when a child's efforts to be his or her own sex go unsupported. Fantasies are fine, but girls must grow up to be women; men can't grow breasts. To lead our children to believe otherwise is unfair and hurtful. If we can avoid the pain children feel when they think their parents don't like the ways they express their femininity or masculinity during childhood, we should, for the ways in which children are girlish or boyish are not permanent. And if we can offer our sons and daughters better resources with which to build their gender identities firmly, we should do that, too. Gender identity *is* permanent.

Does this mean, simply, that nonsexist childrearing is wrong? Yes, in some respects it does. Boys who have difficulty being like the other boys on the block nevertheless need a man who will welcome them into the male world, whether what they share is cooking or football. And if cooking is the basis of sharing, it should stand in contrast to a mother's cooking—concoctions instead of cookies, steaks not quiche. Girls who don't like Barbie dolls nevertheless need attention paid to their feminine qualities, even if all we can compliment is the fit of their jeans or their way with horses. After all, our major worry with atypical children is not whether they will grow up to be gentle men or successful career women, but whether they will enjoy the sex they are enough to keep them from sinking in whirlpools of doubt or crashing against the rocks of anger.

Nonsexist parenting is more a danger to atypical children than it is to typical ones, who, as we have noticed all along, seem awfully good at ignoring ideology. Yet to feminists, that is the greatest danger of all. How will our daughter, if we let her show off her femininity with pink party dresses, become a brain surgeon, they ask? And how will our son take care of babies if he thinks that masculinity begins and ends with cowboy boots? Really, there is nothing to fear. Girls leave the dress-up corner. Boys grow out of cowboy boots. The way they become not only girls and boys, but also grown men and women, continues to unfold.

8

CONSOLIDATION

Most of us would admit that gender confusion is not our goal, but total conformity to gender stereotypes—our baby boy as Burt Reynolds, our baby girl as Suzanne Somers—is not our goal either. Yet at every age, Timmy is taken in by stereotyped come-ons: Wheaties at five, army jackets at ten, *Playboy* centerfolds at fourteen. And girls are no less conventional. Long after the prize of gender identity seems to be won—Timmy and his gang have thrown together a football game and Jennifer giggles endlessly on the phone with her girlfriends—children continue to adhere to conventions we think silly or wrongheaded. Perhaps they have to.

A six-year-old girl or boy is feminine or masculine only in a six-year-old sense. At that age, neither sex is totally convinced that gender is permanent, that they cannot change into the other sex at some later time. Neither girls nor boys can function responsibly as their gender, taking on adult obligations and doing the things men and women do. And six year olds are not functionally heterosexual. Before these first-graders lie another dozen years during which our culture will consider them children and during which they will have to meet the challenges that will make them adult. Now it is masculine for Timmy to collect baseball cards; later it will be masculine for him to step up to bat once more even though he has struck out three times in a row; and later still it will be masculine for him to take his girl out to dinner—and to heck with baseball. Many steps toward full masculinity must be taken and consolidated. All along, stereotypes seem to play a central role.

Liberationists treat this stereotyped behavior as so much dirty water. Their advice is to toss it out, and never mind the baby. But it may be more fruitful to look carefully at children's stereotyped notions for what they can tell us about how the program to achieve a mature gender identity continues to unfold. Since we are concerned about our children's future, we need at least a glimpse of how our babies, now girls and boys, become men and women, for we are worried less by whether Sarah wishes to become a princess now than by whether she can become a professor later. If she can, then it is not the stereotypes that are propaganda, but the advice to toss them out.

Dorothy Ullian, a cognitive psychologist, went straight to the source to discover how children think about gender roles. From the mouths of babes—children from six years old on—it becomes clear that the work a girl or a boy has to go through to become a man or a woman isn't identical with the kind of man or woman he or she becomes. Stereotypes are used, and they are shed, as necessity occasions.[1]

Ullian was curious to discover what children believe distinguishes male from female, man from woman, how children think the sexes ought to be, and how they suppose the sexes could be if circumstances were different. Her method was conversational and open-ended, allowing her and her co-workers to ask a series of standard questions and to pursue novel trains of thought that the researchers could not have anticipated. This open-ended strategy had a singular advantage: it opened Ullian's way to understanding that stereotypes are at least as much sought by children as they are provided by society.

The six year old believes in a biological explanation of sex roles. (Throughout this section, children's levels of conceptualization only roughly correspond to age or grade, from 80 percent of six year olds who have achieved the first level to about 60 percent of college students at the last level. This variation reflects the fact that children differ in the rate at which they arrive at increasingly mature cognitive views; the sequence of stages is more instructive than the exact timing.) Here is a stunning example. The researcher asks whether a women should ever make as much money as a man. "No," the child assures her, "because the man knows how to make more money because a man can do work better than a lady sometimes." Why? "A lady doesn't know so much about working in an insurance agency." Why can't she learn? "Because a father can get more money, the father can do more things than a lady, because, as I was saying, a lady has delicate skin, a man has tougher skin." Women should take care of babies because "the mother's skin is softer than the daddy's skin. And daddies have hair all over their arms and stuff."

We can conceive that this child may have overheard disparaging remarks about women in insurance, but it's absurd to think the adult world has provided footnotes on hairy arms. What's more, this isn't one kid—it's all of them. Six-year-old biological determinism is strange, but unequivocal. Men are big, strong, loud-voiced, and tough-skinned; *therefore* they work, *therefore* they are smart. Women are small, weak, soft-voiced, and smooth-skinned; *therefore* they take care of babies, and since that is not work in the six year old's view, women are not smart. These ideas have no connection to what parents actually do. They come directly from what six year olds see when they look at men and women, fathers and mothers.

First-graders derive not only sex roles from superficial physical characteristics but also psychological qualities, such as smartness (men) and niceness (women). Ullian notes that a particular feature of both boys and girls at this age is their intense admiration for physical labor such as "building houses," "working big machines," and "making roads." Her conversations could not clarify why physical strength and prowess assume such importance to young children. Looking back over earlier years, we can guess that the source is the child's self-generated thrust toward autonomy. His own strivings have long focused on physical and technological feats of all sorts, and Daddy has since infancy been the performer of stunts.

People often think that children are indoctrinated into sex roles through fear of criticism or rejection. Ullian found that this is not true of six year olds. Their preference for convention is clearly their way of ensuring that other people will not mistake them for the wrong sex. What if a girl had short hair, the researcher asks a boy. "She would kind of look like a boy, like I kind of look like a boy. It doesn't look nice if a boy has long hair and a girl has short hair. Because if there is a girl and a boy together, like these two, and say the girl has short hair like the boy, some people would say 'I like these two boys,' but one is really a girl." Another child, asked if boys should play with dolls, replied: "Dolls are what girls like better. It is wrong because then that is like him being kind of like a nurse. Because that is what ladies do, and they might think he was a lady." The fear is not of rejection or criticism; the fear is of being confused with the other sex.

We can understand that gender identity, so connected to the core of self, should be fiercely guarded at this age. The fact that merely conventional trappings of gender—hair, toys, jobs—are guarded emphasizes the difficulty young children have in distinguishing more fundamental characteristics. Like the child who is "not himself" in a new haircut, these young boys and girls are not their own sex without the proper external markings.

These conversational insights help us understand the

children whose obstinate refusal to acknowledge nonsexist roles opened our investigations into the whole subject of gender identity. Women cannot be doctors, even if Mommy *is* a doctor, because they are soft and nice and therefore take care of people, as mothers or nurses do. Doctoring is seen as technical and physical work—thumping chests, hammering knees—which requires the muscles and tough skin of a man. Most important, were a male to wish to become a nurse or a female to wish to become a doctor, that would be "wrong" because it would be confusing. Six year olds, as we have seen, have had enough confusion. We might also note that mothers and fathers play very specific psychological roles in their children's lives; the outsideness of Daddy and the insideness of Mommy are not willingly disrupted by more sophisticated perceptions. No matter how parents may conceive and practice their adult roles, children see their athlete/mother in her nurturing aspect and their nurse/father in his worker aspect. When a teacher assigned her first-grade class to draw stories called "What My Mother Does," Kenneth mentioned only cooking and taking care of children. His mother, a full-time stockbroker, complained at the next PTA meeting, but it wasn't the school's fault. Role sharing and role switching may be an eye-opener to parents, but children remain blind to the implications.

There seems to be little doubt that where society offers first-graders stereotypes that fit their needs, they fairly leap upon them. But, on the other hand, they seem to originate stereotypes all by themselves. Lotion and soap ads notwithstanding, tough skin and delicate skin aren't much emphasized in our society, and it's hard to think of any propaganda at all on the subject of loud and soft voices. Yet it is these characteristics—ones that a newborn baby is wonderfully equipped to notice for himself—from which children derive their stereotyped views of gender roles. The possibility that kids are more complicated than sponges should be kept in mind as we consider the way their stereotyped ideas will blossom in the years to come.

During the years from first grade to college, biological determinism gives way to other determinisms. By ten years old, children think men are smarter not because they work but because they *must* work. "Men are smarter," as one child put it, "because they have to do a lot of things like thinking. They have to work at their jobs. They have to think a lot, and they have to work, and they have to figure things out." Women are now seen to have social obligations that preclude certain kinds of behavior. Aggressiveness, for example, is "wrong" because it is incompatible with childrearing and domestic responsibilities.

The opposing views of children in first and fifth grades are almost a parody of the nature versus nurture controversy, for just as the six year old was convinced that biology is destiny, the ten year old believes that culture is destiny. The social system he has observed is, to him, immutable. He conforms his behavior to what he believes will be his society's rigid and inevitable expectations.

Again, it's not important that his own parents may not fit the rule. He detects the functional pattern of his society— that inherent sexism that gives men their commitment to public roles and women their commitment to private ones— and applies it across the board, just as a child learning to speak will apply language rules consistently and say "I goed" long before he can learn "I went." (We can imagine a certain self-serving quality, too. Women are to mother; children don't particularly wish to see that deadlines and clients might come first.)

At adolescence—somewhere between fourteen and eighteen years old—a new theory of sexual difference emerges. We could call it psychological determinism. Suddenly, masculinity and femininity are viewed as internal psychological differences that are, as Ullian puts it, "independent of, or prior to" sex roles. One adolescent observes that girls "have a lot more emotions on things; I think they have more emotions than men do and they show it more than men do." Such psychological differences now serve to explain the special abilities of each sex: "I think a woman's personality basically is more the type of personality to be staying home with children. Where men's personalities and life style are different. They don't seem to me the type that could sit around, they would probably get bored doing it. With women, it is just something they enjoy doing, if you like kids."

Even teenagers who have avowed feminist beliefs revealed this "true nature" theory of sex differences. One such girl said she would think a man "queer" if he cried in a movie and seemed certain that men handle things better because they are less sensitive than women or show emotions less. Although a girl might act boyish (provided she was not at a dinner party, where she should be "ladylike") her response to a boy acting feminine was, "I wouldn't go near him. Ugh! . . . They must have something wrong with them, maybe they were brought up that way, because they shouldn't act feminine; that is our identity, that is our position, not theirs. They should be masculine. Because that is the way it is always—men are masculine and women are feminine—if they were feminine it would really be strange."

Despite their intellectual grasp of the potential discrepancy between sex stereotypes and the true self, they aren't prepared to agree with Letty Pogrebin that traditional concepts of masculinity and femininity should be abolished. The only true self they consider authentic or normal is that which conforms to standard ideas of masculinity or femininity. Those who do not conform to standards are abnormal or inauthentic; they are not "being themselves." Psychological determinism is every bit as rigid as biological or social determinism, and just as conventional.

As each new basis for stereotypes emerges during childhood, we can identify a specific challenge that seems aptly served by the child's conclusions. At the first-grade level, when the child concludes that gender roles are generated by physical characteristics, he is under internal pressure to firm up his gender identity, to make sure it is permanent. Since he doesn't have the physical characteristics themselves (all children have soft skins and high voices), he adopts the actions he thinks they generate. This is the age of heartbreaking stereotypes—skinny boys in cowboy boots, gawky girls in tutus. Later, the challenge shifts to an external one: responsibilities that school-age children are expected to take seriously and that are considered preparatory to adult obligations. We find this stage wonderful, for it supplies us with reliable mothers' helpers and ardent lawn mowers. We—and they—are often thrown for a loop when, in adolescence, these sane and co-operative children peel out into the inane stereotypes of budding heterosexuality. Their source is eclectic. One mother, who had survived the latest codes in punk, pot, and slang, was astonished to find her son buying a sweetheart rose corsage and renting a tux to take his girl to the senior prom.

However, as each of these determinisms gives way to new views of the world, the child goes through an apparently liberal phase before entrenching himself in the next determinism. Children who have given up biological determinism temporarily think it's okay for a boy to sew doll clothes like a girl, and for a girl to throw footballs like a boy. Their effort to consolidate their sense of self and gender identity has worked. Very little kids scare themselves by putting on a Halloween mask, but eight year olds enjoy it. Their sense of being themselves can survive external changes of appearance. They feel similarly assured that their gender identity will remain constant. At this age, boys and girls may wear nearly identical, unisex clothing; they can *be* their sex without *doing* their sex.

Liberal indoctrination seems to play as flimsy a part in this transient "liberalism" as conventional indoctrination played in the conventional beliefs of younger children. One girl, when asked what she would think of a woman with big muscles, replied: "I don't think it's nice, well, I think it's all right. What's the matter with having big muscles? I'm always lifting things for my mother and father, and my mother says, you shouldn't do that. Well, there's nothing the matter with it. I'm not trying to be fresh with her, but I don't think there is anything the matter with it." Similarly, most third-graders agree that there is nothing wrong with a boy wanting to become a nurse, even in the face of parental disapproval: "It is not really his father's choice, if he wanted to be it. His father can't tell him not to."

This liberalism fades away as the child mobilizes his gender identity in the service of responsible functioning. Again, as he achieves this new level of gender consolidation, the child lets up on himself and once more appears liberated from strict constraints.

Most twelve year olds appreciate that the social order they observe, and that they once thought inevitable, is an outcome of relatively arbitrary traditions. Asked which sex he thought was smarter, one boy expressed this new sophistication: "I think when you get twenty-five, it starts changing. Men just start learning stuff in college too, because they want to get a good job, and they really start to learn stuff. It depends, right now I think women are smarter, but later men will be smart. There is no real difference to who is smarter. If you want to be smart, you can be smart by learning more, but if women wanted to get a job, I am sure they are just as smart as men are."

This second liberal interval, too, is short-lived.

The challenge of heterosexual functioning comes hard on its heels, and with it the rigid theory of psychological determinism. Supported by the constraints he now imagines to be an aspect of his authentic nature, the adolescent is enabled to enter the heterosexual social world. After a few more years of experience in integrating that aspect of gender identity as well, the young adult sheds belief in all determinisms.

Whereas the younger teenagers Ullian interviewed thought that heterosexual relations had to be governed by stereotype, most college students see heterosexuality as mediated through the same values that mediate all other human relationships. Traditional sex roles are no longer seen as fundamental either to personal identity or to heterosexual functioning. "Personally," said one young man, "the ideal woman to me can be beautiful, and soft, but the ideal man may also be soft in the same way, because he is soft-spoken, not domineering over anyone, but still with ambition to get things done." Our college-bound sons and daughters are breezy on the subject of working wives and nurturing husbands. Parents who harp on traditional sex roles and themes are asking for trouble. More than at any other stage, stereotyped sex differences are disparaged as behaviors learned in childhood from an unjust society—or from old-fashioned parents.

The funny thing is, parents don't seem to have much to do with how conventional or unconventional their college-age children turn out to be. The whole theory of nonsexist childrearing rests on an assumption that if a family can rid itself of traditional sex roles, the children will grow up free of stereotyped behavior. The fact is that there seems to be no relationship whatsoever between the stereotyped behavior of parents and that of their college-age children. One study, conducted by B. G. Rosenberg and Brian Sutton-Smith, focused on college women from two-child families.[2] The women, their fathers, mothers, sister, or brother were given the Gough Femininity Scale, which rates individuals with respect to stereotyped sex-role behavior.

The college women's scores did not relate in any way to that of their mothers' or fathers', nor did their brother's or sister's scores. Daughters of committed housewives are as likely to want careers as daughters of women executives are likely to put marriage and children first. Scholars can raise soccer players just as truckers can raise poets.

Similar studies have been done with children of preschool, kindergarten, and first-grade ages. The results were the same. There simply is no evidence that a child's masculine or feminine behavior is modeled on any stereotypes parents may present. Daughters of den mothers don't all love crafts and cooking. Sons of such women are also no more interested in sewing and cooking than another child, nor does a father who does all the home repairs manage to interest all his children in pipes and lumber. Perhaps we parents don't have to share in fixing cars and frying chicken, if it is only to make a point to our children. Perhaps we don't have to live up to their conventional ideas of what mommies and daddies are like either.

There even seems to be some doubt that parents *use* the stereotypes they hold. Wallace E. Lambert and his colleagues, working with Canadian parents, presented their subjects with a list of forty characteristics such as "more likely to act scared," "more helpful around the house," "more likely to act rough and boisterous in play."[3] The parents were asked to decide which items more accurately described boys or girls and which items applied equally to both sexes. The result matched well with the stereotypes we're all familiar with. Boys were described as rougher, noisier, more active, more competitive, more likely to enjoy mechanical things and participate in dangerous activities. Girls were described as more helpful, neat, clean, quiet, well mannered, easily upset and frightened, and sensitive to the needs of others.

That established, Lambert went on to ask the parents to rate each of the now sex-linked items on a five-point scale from "very important to" to "very important not to," with the midpoint being "unimportant." The picture changed completely. Parents, thinking now in terms of what boys and girls *should* be like rather than their perception of what children *are* like, made few distinctions between the sexes. They thought both boys and girls should be neat, clean, and helpful around the house. They thought neither sex should cry, act scared, or lose their temper easily. They felt both boys and girls should be competitive and should fight back if they were attacked.

Given this difference between parents' descriptive and prescriptive judgments, how does that difference relate to the ways adults actually raise children? Maccoby and Jacklin report a rather large group of studies conducted by question-naire, personal interview, and home observation that have sought to find ways in which parents and teachers encourage children to conform to stereotypes. Specifically, the research-ers postulated that if we equate masculinity with aggressive-ness, we will encourage aggressive behavior in boys by punishing it less, rewarding it more, or at least permitting it to happen. If Tom blacks Bobby's eye, his parents should give him a good talking to instead of whaling his backside, or they should say, "I'm proud of you, son," or they should just overlook the incident. But when Jessica blacks Bobby's eye, her parents should act horrified. Perhaps only the psycholo-gists were surprised when this did not turn out to be the case. Mothers and fathers curtail aggression with both sons and daughters. Most parents would have guessed that—but might have added, "unless the other kid deserved a punch in the nose."

A few of the studies found differences between mothers and fathers. A mother seems to be a bit more tolerant of her son's aggressive behavior when it is directed toward herself and a father may permit greater "insolence" toward himself by a daughter. Fathers in general come down harder than mothers on a boy's aggressiveness; they discourage it. Female teachers, far from discouraging female aggression and toler-ating male aggression, reprimand boys more severely for ag-gressive behavior and respond to boys' aggressive acts more frequently even when girls are behaving identically. In most of the studies, no difference was found in how adults respond to a boy's or a girl's aggression toward themselves, valued objects, siblings, or peers. If aggression or the lack of it is a sex stereotype, adults don't seem to make any attempt to shape children to fit it.

Nevertheless, sex stereotypes are the salient features in our imagery of sex differences. They are surprisingly uniform between sexes, across socioeconomic classes, at varying ages, in disparate cultures, and even over long spans of historic time. If they do not function as models for real-life behavior, and if we do not or cannot shape our children to fit them, what in the world are sex stereotypes for?

Sex stereotypes are for marking the boundaries between the sexes so that such boundaries will not be stepped over by mistake. Like ethnic or class stereotypes, they serve to separate the identities of two groups, emphasizing the more evident features of one identity by opposing it to the more evident features of the other. When both groups share each other's stereotypes, as is usually the case, each maintains self-esteem by applying a plus sign to those stereotypes that distinguish its own group and a negative sign to the other. Tom and Jessica will agree that boys are rough, but Tom will grin about it and Jessica will wrinkle her nose.

Stereotypes are like an alphabet, a distinctive model by which we can identify an "A" or a "B" no matter in what idiosyncratic style it is written, even if it deviates extremely from the model. Sex stereotypes do not concern themselves with subtleties or even reflect reality. The masculine stereotype, for example, does not insist that only men become artists, even though most of the great artists in our history have been male. Like billboards along a highway, they flash the most visible and most simple-minded images. The emphasis, moreover, is not on conformity but on contrast. It is less important that a man fit the male stereotype than that he not merge into the female stereotype. No woman really feels that she must sob often and be afraid of bugs to be feminine; but she may well feel that to win at the expense of others is discordant with her view of herself as female or might be perceived as masculine by men. What sex stereotypes seem to tell us is that it is terribly important to males and females that they remain distinct from one another; sex-role determinism and the stereotypes it supports act as signposts, not as scripts, for the full development of gender identity. Whether generated by the child or supplied by society (probably it is both), they are picked up when needed and may be discarded when the need is less pressing.

Then is the college student's sex-blind value system the ultimate stage of sex-role conceptualization? Ullian suggests that it is, yet it has all the earmarks of previous interphases that were merely respites before life's demands urged another set of constraints and a more integrated level of gender identity. This new value system, while adamantly espoused, was not so easy for the students Ullian talked to to apply in their own personal lives. A marriage in which the wife was breadwinner or decision-maker seemed valid and even admirable, but at the same time men and women at this stage were not sure they wanted such a marriage or could respond warmly to a lover who defied traditional expectations. They should not care if wives work but they did. They should not care if husbands are shorter or less intelligent, but they did. Moreover, there is a foretaste of a new determinism in their remarks. The question is: Who should take care of the kids?

> I don't know. I think that right now, I have not had enough psychology to know if you took a child away from its mother and let the father take care of it, whether there would be any adverse effects or not, I don't know about that, there might be. Until some type of test is made, I would think that there would be, because I have never seen anything else and it has never happened so I would think that a child, at least for a while, should be kept with the mother. I am not sure if there is a special relationship between a child and a mother.[4]

With the wisdom of hindsight, most of us know that the next great challenges facing these young men and women are adult work and the particular love relationships of marriage and childrearing. There is no name as yet for the sense of determinism that will come over them, but it will be there. Few of the women will choose to pursue their careers during the months following the birth of their first baby. Most of them will be taken by surprise by what almost amounts to a nest-building urge to clean, repaint, and remodel their homes as the birth approaches. They, who never sewed a button, may suddenly want to knit. When their babies are born, they will find themselves bored by corporate decisions and company gossip—by nearly everything about the outside world. Nothing will be able to compete with the grip of a tiny hand, the flash of a baby's smile. Caring for their child will be an astounding pleasure these women will not interrupt without reluctance. Women, for all their many theories about sex roles, will feel a completeness that feminist principles did not predict. And almost none of the men will choose to stay at home. For all their willingness to try out cooking and for all the delight their babies will give them, they will find most of their satisfactions in the work of the outside world.

All along, we have posited that psychological and intellectual development must be seen as outcomes of an interactional program. Fine tuning occurs, but the rough outlines are an evolutionary heritage over which we have little control. In an evolutionary sense, the consolidation of gender identity through all the vicissitudes of infancy, childhood, adolescence, and young adulthood can serve only one ultimate purpose: the rearing of the next generation.

As our children begin to raise babies of their own, we can perceive that the program is sensible. Without the soft, blurred boundaries with which our daughters are endowed, how could they let their babies into themselves, feel their needs from inside, and nurture them with their own bodies? Without the separateness with which our sons are endowed, how could they keep all sorts of needs and demands from impinging on the task at hand? Women must be interruptible so that babies can interrupt them. Men must be aloof from interruption so that their jobs get done. In this ancient partnership, the ancient differences work well.

We are now in a position to look at these differences without bias. The feminist accusation that we live in a male-dominated society is certainly true in the sense that male and female alike share a masculine bias. Even very young children have an admiration for masculine "work" they may never have been taught. More crucial to our perspective here is bias exhibited by the researchers whose child development data and interpretation we rely upon. From Freud to feminist, researchers have attempted to discern a single developmental scale by which both sexes might be measured. Those scales reveal a masculine bias.

Maturity, for example, is taken to mean autonomy and achievement. Working backward from that goal, various developmental milestones that support ultimate autonomy and achievement have been identified. Those people who fail to reach the last milestone are considered to have fallen short of maturity. They are usually female.

The appalling error in this sort of thinking is the assumption that males and females grow up experiencing reality in the same ways and should therefore arrive at the same end point. Thus, the fact that girls do not separate from their mothers as completely as boys, do not experience their selves as independently, do not arrive at an abstract basis for moral judgments, and do not seek success in competitive terms points to frankly stunted development—to Freudians because nature made females that way, to feminists because society did. In both views, girls seemed to deviate from the "normal" boys' scheme.

Only recently has the development of girls and boys from infancy onward been studied in enough detail to challenge this bias. The experience of being a girl is simply not like the experience of being a boy. The story of each opens in a different setting, proceeds according to a different plot, and comes to its own unique conclusion. Though many of the words are the same, they have contrasting meanings. The word "game" is taken by males to mean a venture that transcends the players. Proceeding by rule is paramount and legalistic negotiations often require as much attention as the play itself. To females, games are subordinate to the human attachments they express; rules are there to bring rewards to everyone, and when they fail to do so, the game itself is forfeited. Neither the game nor the rules that govern it have a role independent of the players. Male morality appeals to principles that are above the sufferings or triumphs of the individuals involved—"blind" justice. Female morality is more pragmatic; what is moral is what hurts all the parties the least and meets their needs the best, regardless of compromise to principles. Male success is measured by the position society accords the successful man. Females measure success in broader terms—by how their body of work has affected other people.

It is impossible to imagine a society in which one or the other set of values was abandoned. Morality fails without compromise as it fails without principles. Success unheralded by position is unrewarding, as success that has left others unaffected is empty. Most crucial, babies cannot be raised without a woman's talent for sustaining closeness, without her comforting and humane morality, or her willingness to measure her children subjectively, by whatever is the best that child can do. Nor can a baby be raised without a man's encouraging distance, his inspiring transcendence, or his enticing otherness. Each generation of babies is endowed with self by both parents, and parenting is the future that our boys and girls, now proclaiming their freshman nonsexism, seem to have been preparing for all along.

The good news is that we need not worry when our daughter wants to become a princess or our son a truck driver. Early understanding of gender role has as little to do with adult masculinity and femininity as a child's understanding of nature or anatomy has to do with adult science. Nonsexist upbringing will not short-circuit the built-in developmental sequence of sex-role concepts, nor will sexist upbringing freeze the sequence in some early stage. Young adults, regardless of their family's ideology, seem touchingly prepared for parenthood even as they are poised to turn in novel directions.

The bad news is that the world in which the intricate human scheme of development evolved is changing. Women, so precisely fashioned to provide a continuance of attachment, intimacy, and empathy from one generation to another, are under pressure to become more separated than the nature of many easily allows. And men, so early realizing the distance and separation that turns them to the outside world, are being asked to experience a closeness very difficult for many of them to endure.

The period of intense childrearing for which evolution has shaped our gifts is shrinking. As the number of children in each family decreases and as longevity increases, that period will take up only a scant portion of a person's life. If the ancient scheme that has so well prepared these young adults to be parents is to be needed for only a few years, is it fair that their whole lives should be affected? Are our sons and daughters to suffer from their gifts forever?

9

TOMORROW'S CHILDREN

From generation to generation, in ours or any other culture, the traditions of childrearing support a child's own efforts to achieve a distinct gender identity and to live as a mature man or woman. Liberated parents defy these traditions in the belief that they cause boys and girls to suffer from too narrow concepts of how men and women should act. By discouraging stereotypes of masculinity and femininity, many such families hope to produce children who are not bound by the limits of those traditions, who will be able to participate more fully in one another's contrasting experiences of self, relationship, role, and work. When these social experiments are confined to providing role-breaking examples—sharing in domestic routines and economic support—or to liberated choices in books, toys, schools, and ideologies, the experiment is probably making little headway and is also doing very little harm.

Compared to the world views children themselves generate, these things are superficial. As long as the fundamental "grammar" of the society can be discerned by children, they will ignore the exceptions. And as long as the relationships from which infants first derive their earliest understanding of gender—the game as it is played by mothers and by fathers, the smells, touches, sounds, and movements that tell them who and what they are—are not tampered with, they will grow up pretty much as they do now.

But social experiment can—and has—gone further than these superficials. Whole societies, by treating their babies with distance and discomfort, have been made masculine. Whole societies, by treating their babies without any distance or any discomfort, have been made feminine. Large populations of children, by being denied any intense parenting, have grown to adulthood with just the lack of clear distinctions between the sexes that nonsexism advocates. For every such shift, there are repercussions that are not easy to predict and results that we may not desire. Before we embark on any drastic course that may produce definitive results, we had best study the voyages of other adventurers or find our own steady stars to guide us.

Margaret Mead, the anthropologist, is a heroine to feminists because her work showed that temperament is independent of gender. In one society she studied, our own Western description of femininity fit both sexes; in another, our description of masculinity fit both sexes. Mead describes in some detail the infancy and childhoods of both these groups and, although less research had been done in the psychology of child development in the 1930's, it was apparent to Mead that the extreme childrearing traditions and the extremes of temperament she observed were related. Radical departures from what is usual in our own society had been achieved by exaggerating either the baby's experience of continuity with his mother or the baby's experience of distance from his mother. Inner distance or the lack of it then defined the growing child's actual relationships with others, and this inner model was reflected in and supported by the institutions of the culture.

Briefly, Arapesh babies were kept in a soft net bag against their mother's body throughout infancy and were gratified almost before their needs were expressed. This refusal to frustrate, scold, or withhold continued throughout childhood. Signs of aggression were gentled over by distraction, feeding, and cuddling. The outcome was adults who were capable of exquisite cooperation. There was no concept of ownership, individuality, or independence in Arapesh society. Each person was fed by others and fed others. No Arapesh ever grew any food for his own use. Perhaps among no other peoples has the human capacity for mutuality been so sharpened or the human capacity for aggression been so blunted.

Mead, while delighting in these gentle people, was astonished to note that they were incapable of invention. Even minor innovations—a new dance step or style of bracelet—were imported from neighboring tribes. Everyday leadership was elusive. A leader chosen to search out new trade contacts or resolve disputes did so with a show of reluctance and disengagement; he could act only "as if" he were aggressive. No individual took responsibility for direct, competitive, angry, or self-serving actions. Mead herself, while satisfied by this proof that "masculine" temperament is not inherent to males, mused on the vulnerability of such a culture. The Arapesh lacked the capacity either to progress through their own innovation or to mobilize in their own defense.

The Mundugumor, in contrast, raised their children with a distance so chilling as to seem cruel. They hung their babies in scratchy baskets and left them to cry themselves into a rage before suckling them briefly, pinioned in an awkward position under the exasperated mother's arm. Male and female alike grew up untrusting, remote, and mean. Aggression was more than intact—it permeated every routine of daily living from eating meals to having sex. There was a quality of perpetual violating of others. The Mundugumors' independence amounted, in fact, to divisiveness. Life's warm pleasures—coziness, intimacy, sympathy, mutuality—were simply absent.

Feminists have been triumphant about Mead's work because they feel it proves there are no fundamental differences between the sexes. Men can have qualities we expect to find in women, and women can be like men; it is entirely a matter of culture and upbringing. But Mead herself claimed, and the work of other anthropologists confirms, that no culture that has been examined fails to make fundamental distinctions between men and women and to express those distinctions in the symbols and structure of their society. Most interesting in the light of our present discussion, those distinctions seem to be just the ones that our sophisticated and diverse culture makes. Arapesh leaders, no matter how reluctant, were always male. Their central public institution, a ritual feasting, was planned and carried out by men. Their shamlike confrontations were all male. Among the violent Mundugumor, aggression was nevertheless regulated through rigid protocols—but only for males. Females, as girls and women, were allowed a much freer social life without the restrictions of a complex hierarchy and the ritualized encounters that marshaled all male contacts. But women played no part in ceremonial life, except as audience. In both cultures, girls and boys were early distinguished by clothes, ornaments, and tools that signified their sex.

Even where, as in these extreme societies, differences in temperament have been blurred to the point of invisibility, men throw the spears and women carry the baskets. Public life, hierarchical affiliation, and institutionalized aggression remain masculine domains, as domestic life, egalitarian groups, and informality remain the female way of doing things. These stubborn distinctions constitute the meaning of male and female, and ensure that boys and girls understand their sexual identity in contrasting ways so that even people with the most similar temperaments express their gender through different forms. Uniformity of temperament does not destroy gender identity.

What is destroyed in cultures that have taken extreme swings toward a uniformly masculine or feminine temperament is adaptability. Unlike our own culture, in which each family raises its babies in somewhat different ways, all families in small homogeneous cultures like the Arapesh and Mundugumor bring up babies in the same way. While this ensures that no Arapesh will be independent and thus unable to share food, and no Mundugumor will be dependent and thus unable to grab food, such cultures cannot easily shift to different behaviors should occasion demand. How would the Arapesh galvanize their men for war if it were necessary? Who would step forth to lead them to a new land or to invent a new technology if this were necessary? The Mundugumor are just as vulnerable. Their divisiveness leaves no room for abeyance of self or commitment to a group venture should their present way of life fail them. A culture that changes by adopting extremely masculinizing or extremely feminizing parenting is taking a great risk.

We do not know whether the adoption of extreme child-rearing practices among these peoples was the result of a mere drift toward this or that way of raising babies that happened to fit the vicissitudes of an environment, or whether the environment implacably eradicated individuals who were not so raised. It is doubtful that conscious choice entered into the original adaptation. Today, however, aided by knowledge of child development, societies do make conscious choices. A clear example is the kibbutz movement in Israel, which was founded on socialist principles and later fueled by the survivors of the Holocaust who brought with them to the promised land a distrust of the close family traditions of the ghetto. Their idea was to raise children communally so that they would work together with strength and would not be sapped by the sentimentality of family life.

Kibbutz babies and children live with their peers in children's houses run by metapelahs whose lives are entirely devoted to child care. A metapelah takes care of a single age group so that infants "graduate" from their babyhood metapelah to the one who cares for toddlers, or of preschoolers or of an older group. Thus, it is not the care-giver but the peer group that remains stable, for the whole "crop" of babies is moved as a unit from house to house as they grow. The ratio of metapelahs to children does not allow for quick, careful, or prolonged attention to minor hurts or wishes. Very early, the children begin to do for one another, and the peer group in many ways replaces nurturing functions usually associated with parents. Parents do maintain a special relationship with their sons and daughters, but the busy communal and pragmatic life of a kibbutz precludes any great investment of time and emotion.

In his book *Children of the Dream*, Bruno Bettelheim examined the psychological outcomes of communal rearing on Israeli kibbutzim.[1] Without the intimacy and exclusiveness intensive parenting provides, Bettelheim found kibbutz children in general happier but flatter than their American counterparts. They felt less need for individuality, were more content with cooperation, and were rarely caught up in grave conflict, depression, or confusion. Sexual equality was a way of life. Personal relationships, however, struck Bettelheim as rather matter-of-fact, lacking in depth or passion. Although the children he studied performed admirably in school, there was a leveling influence. Failure and giftedness were both rare; curiosity seemed dulled. Among teenagers, sexual relations were considered natural and accepted with little comment, and yet these relations had a perfunctory quality, as though they were not of great moment. Homosexuality was rare, but heterosexuality was blunted.

Bettelheim did not find that communal rearing of children caused confusion in gender identity. Most parents chose to spend what time they could afford with their infants and children, and the metapelahs, too, gave boys and girls that modicum of differentiation that supports the growth of gender identity. What was lacking was intensity: intensity of either closeness or distance and, especially, intense love relationships with adults. Gender identity as it is expressed by the children of the dream is a stripped-down version, bare of the elaborate richness and variety produced in the fussy factory of family life.

Nevertheless, nonsexism grows well in this flat landscape. The children of the dream may be the most androgynous population in the world and may also predict the results we ourselves might achieve if we were to embrace on a national scale another feminist goal: communal infant and child care.

This thoughtful work of Mead, Bettelheim, and others forces us to recognize that masculinity and femininity are not absolutes; they are a matter of degree. We can picture a long scale at one end of which is a very pliant and giving feminine temperament and at the other end of which is a very stern and distant masculine temperament. On such a scale, the Arapesh—males and females—are shifted way to one end, while the Mundugumor of both sexes are shifted to the other end. We can place the children who grow up on kibbutzim to one side of center, somewhat toward the detached, masculine end.

This scale also helps us to visualize the total range of gender roles available to both sexes and to think about the overlap between the sexes. In both the Arapesh and the Mundugumor cultures, the total range of gender roles is very small while the overlap is rather large. There are few slots to fill, and most can be filled by both sexes. The range of gender role in kibbutz culture is moderate, and the overlap is also very great. There's a greater choice of what to be in life, and almost any role that one sex can take on, the other sex can too.

There are also societies—traditional Arab culture is one example—in which the range of gender role is moderate but in which there is almost no overlap between the area occupied by males and the area occupied by females.

These three measures—shift, range, and overlap—are useful concepts in examining our future potential as we continue to struggle with our nonsexist ideals and the very real pressures that are heaped upon us. Were we to place ourselves along the scale, we would have to recognize that we occupy a central position, shifted neither toward the extremes of masculinity nor toward the extremes of femininity. Our range of gender role is very broad; there are many things for men and women to do and be in our heterogeneous and pluralistic society. Moreover, we enjoy an unusually large overlap in comparison with other cultures. Already accustomed to a degree of freedom for both sexes, we are unlikely to want any change in childrearing practices that threatens to shift the entire population toward a more masculine or a more feminine expression, to shrink the total domain we occupy to a narrower range of roles, or to decrease the overlap between the sexes. Rather, we would wish to maintain our central position, perhaps expand our total range, and certainly increase our overlap.

Neither of the two anthropological models we have proposed will meet these goals. If we masculinize or feminize all or most of our babies, we will shift the entire population off-center and leave ourselves vulnerable to changes that we cannot predict and will be unable to control. If we lessen the intensity of our parenting, we will narrow our children's potential at both ends by stultifying individualism and creativity on the one hand and pliable pragmatism on the other. We cannot leave our destiny to unconscious drift, although we probably cannot prevent some drifting. And we dare not trust only to conscious plans the outcome of which may hold unpleasant surprises.

There is another mechanism of social change that best describes what already appears to be happening in our own society, whether or not unconscious drift or conscious planning is simultaneously adding to the momentum. Paradoxically, the mechanism relies on the nonsexist ideals so frequently called into question in the course of our story but which will now emerge as the clarion call of our conclusion.

The virtue of nonsexist parenting is that it implants an enduring value system. In studies similar to those in which the effects of stereotyped sex roles have been examined, researchers have found that values absorbed in childhood link parents with their children across the generations. When a child is brought up to value honesty, fairness, persistence, or peace, those ideals permeate his world view, color his experience, and guide him in adult conduct. The boys and girls Ullian interviewed are clearly gripped by the nonsexist values their family or our culture has taught them. Whether or not their parents pushed a shovel or pushed a pen, worked at a desk or worked at the kitchen sink, did not seem to affect their attitudes. But each time a new gain in maturity released these children from a narrowed understanding of sex roles, their views hovered close to the liberated ideal. Children from an earlier era or a stricter culture could not have held this ideal. Our children are learning it now, here, from us. Nonsexist childrearing cannot create boys and girls free to bloom with all the flowerings of human potential. But the feminist ideal will create people of both sexes free to explore in novel ways the rich capacities of their own gender and, in many ways, to expand them.

Originally we looked at biology to explain the constraints evolution has placed upon our species. Now we must look at biology again to understand the freedom from constraint that our species enjoys. So far, we have viewed the interactional program whereby neutral babies come to be masculine or feminine in terms of familiar and universal outcomes that evolved because they served reproduction. Now we must see the program as a transforming dynamic by which human adaptation over a very broad sphere is accomplished.

Letty Pogrebin, that outspoken advocate of nonsexist childrearing, says: "Masculinity and femininity do not exist. They are fictions. . . . "[2] In one way, she is quite right. Although they are not the fictions she claims, they are also not things, entities to be found in one sex but not in the other. Masculinity and femininity are capacities, or, rather, they are two aspects of a single capacity to generate rules

expression of what it is like to be a little girl. That's what it means to have a capacity, and not a thing. Masculinity and femininity are creative expressions of the constraint of being one's sex.

At every age, individuals select from the entire culture what is interesting to them at that point or serves their needs best. In doing so, they transform the very culture from which they made their selection. The ingredients may be as different from the final product as eggs and cheese are from a soufflé. The children of the sexual revolution transformed free sex into an utterly novel living arrangement: male and female roommates who *don't* sleep together. This sort of reciprocity has been built into human beings throughout our life cycle. Culture makes us; we, in turn, make culture.

When we left Ullian's children, eighteen and twenty now, they were poised on the brink of conflict. That blue jean generation had come to respect, as we had intended it to respect, the feminist ideal. But these boys and girls have not yet solved the problem of how they will incorporate their ideals into their everyday lives. Their very quandary is the stuff of social change as it is being practiced now in our culture. At no time in our lives are we quite so eager or quite so able to mold our culture to our own ends as in young adulthood.

Adolescence is a barely noticeable phenomenon in less developed cultures. The passage from childish dependence to adult responsibility is marked by rituals that symbolize psychic growth, but there is no prolonged period during which the individual is considered to be between childhood and adulthood. Though we often disparage and misunderstand it, we ourselves, by nurturing individualism and autonomy almost from infancy, have brought the phenomenon to full flower in our culture. The degree of separation we ask of our children is a great challenge. But by giving our sons and daughters the wherewithal to meet our expectations, we have unleashed a powerful capacity for cultural invention.

The process of emerging from childhood is in many ways a replay of the process of emerging from infancy. The baby stems his limbs against his mother to seek a more distant view and thereby finds himself. The teenager, too, pushes off from his parents to seek new perspectives and thereby finds his individuality. Again, as the toddler stabilizes his sense of self by incorporating the views of others, the adolescent becomes increasingly concerned with how others see him. Toddlers are able to counteract any loss of self-esteem that is brought about by objectivity by mastering their environment, by doing for themselves and winning their parents' support on their own terms. So, too, teenagers shore up their shaky self-esteem by exercising their autonomy.

But now a child's understanding of the arena in which he can be effective is greatly expanded. As parents who have come through their children's teenage years recognize, adolescents do not easily yield to situations that do not suit them. They press for change within the family, and often they get it. They negotiate new rules, force accommodations to their schedules, and bend family relationships into shapes consistent with their needs. The unusual pressure we place upon our children to be individuals and to act independently—those new, rare values in the world—fills these years with furious battles and contrite tears, an ambivalence that is the very flavor of our teenage drama.

In spite of the fact that the intensities of adolescence tend to obscure the working out of gender identity, the unfolding is still at work. A boy's "rebellion" is a necessary outcome of his struggle for individuality. The typically more stormy adolescence of girls is evidence of their continuing ambivalence regarding separation. Adolescent drama is a measure of how separated we ask our kids to be. Perhaps even our impatience and irritation with teenagers originates in their struggle. As long as we don't squelch them entirely or force them out into the world too soon, parental unpleasantness is needed to loosen our children's ties to us.

For both sexes, the loosening of childlike bonds to parents is accompanied, as was the shedding of infantile bonds, by more mature forms of attachment. Teenagers gradually become more able to love us for all our faults and to invest the passion of their earliest years in heterosexual relationships outside the family. "Falling in love" is written into the time-table; it occurs on schedule independently of the hormonal goings-on of adolescence and the ability to produce children, although the two roughly coincide for most people. The desire to have a mate is, of course, a point of the whole program we have been tracing from infancy.

But the program doesn't grind to a halt at the age of twenty. We continue all through our lives to experience changes in our feelings about ourselves and how we express them, in our relationships with people, in our abilities, and even in our gender identities. These youngsters, poised to turn in novel directions, are readying themselves not only to have a mate and have babies but to raise those babies in an uncertain future. This has been true of every generation of new parents. Perhaps you recall your own grandparents fussing about new-fangled ways of raising "you kids," and maybe now your parents recall how you were raised, in the days before nonsexist nonsense. The fact is that your grandparents changed the institution of the family somewhat to fit their world, and so did your parents, and you, and so will your children. The future is never a given. Adolescence particularly prepares children to deal with what their parents can't teach them and their neurons don't know. The whole period is marked by a prodigious spurt in intellectual growth.

Younger children are unable to take part in formal debates because they can only take the "right" side of an argument. But teenagers are able to argue any side of an issue, delighting as much in the merit of the argument or the novel perspective it affords as in the rightness or wrongness of their view. Everything seems possible; they discover Utopia. Not too successfully at first, but still with verve, adolescents begin to take on the actual institutions of their culture: education, religion, law, and custom. Within a few years, their ability to effect cultural transformation is sharpened. The 1960s affords us an emphatic example of just how well and how rapidly our children, as they enter their twenties, can invent new cultural forms.

The phenomenon of youth as the trigger of social change is another of evolution's gifts, and it is not confined to the human species. Some years ago, it was the custom of a group of Japanese macaque monkeys to clean sweet potatoes of annoying grit by wiping them with their hands.[3] One brilliant young female invented a better method—washing sweet potatoes in the surf. The pattern by which this cultural novelty eventually permeated macaque society is instructive: first (and fast) the other adolescents appreciated the innovation, followed more slowly by their mothers, who taught it to younger children. The adult males of that generation never did accept this "radical" idea. Only when they had died and a new generation had taken on adult roles was the invention accepted as a by now "conservative" method of cleaning sweet potatoes.

In human culture, as in ape culture, today's radicals are tomorrow's conservatives. Evolution suggests a life cycle of checks and balances in which the older members of a society—perhaps males in particular—preserve culture as it has worked for them, while youthful members (could it be females in particular?) adopt new ways that may work better for themselves in the future. At the time of the Declaration of Independence, Hamilton was twenty-one, Jefferson thirty-three, Jay thirty-one, and Madison twenty-five. Had the radical revolution led by those youngsters failed, older conservatives would still have been around to guide a new generation. On the other hand, if younger members of society never prevailed, there would be no cultural advance. History, among men and apes alike, is progressive. The Japanese macaques progressed from washing their sweet potatoes in the shallow sea to using it as the source of a new food, seaweed. The United States went on to forge a new version of democracy.

When we realize that young men and women, while constrained by the imperatives of their gender identity, are also the powerhouse for change in our society, we can be sanguine about the future of feminism. Today, as both sexes struggle to resolve the conflicting schedules of getting educated, advancing in a career, and raising babies, they will change the timing of all these events to meet their needs. As they find today's centralized offices at commuting distances uncongenial to their goals, they will reshape the distinction between home and workplace. And as they discover that existing institutions are incompatible with their own most effective ways of doing things, they will change the very ways those institutions function. Already changes in timing, location, and function are visible—adult education, later marriage, convenience foods, parental leaves of absence, rural branch offices and plants, job sharing, on-site day care, and home computer terminals.

These first gropings toward a solution—clumsy, inconvenient, and personally trying as they often are—set the stage for more radical transformations. For as women move, however imperfectly and slowly, into the public institutions of our culture, their effect is profound. We have only to think of how children's education as it is conducted now by female teachers is nothing like education as it used to be conducted by male teachers. Surely medicine as it is practiced now cannot remain the same as more women become doctors. The different understandings of friendship and play that females experience will have their effect on corporate ways. Our system of justice, our concept of government, the rules by which we guide our society will certainly change as more women become lawyers, judges, administrators, and politicians.

The question of whether women can "make it" in the man's world of council halls and corporations is a false question. For when either sex enters a territory once the exclusive province of the other, it changes the territory in as palpable a manner as women's entry into political life changed the issues that were addressed or men's entry into midwivery changed the procedures of childbirth. As each is successful, success is redefined.

Over the course of this century, we have spiraled upward to see our genders in a new light. At first, thinking of masculinity as a stuff that could be measured and that brought rewards in proportion with the amount of it a person had, women thought that in all fairness they deserved to have more of it, so they could measure themselves and receive rewards in kind. But what delights a man has not proven delightful to all women. Some women have not found corporate politics fun or even enlightening. They have discovered that and many other aspects of masculine endeavor to be rather beside the point, a parallel way of getting to goals, but one that is not their way. They would do things differently, and they have.

Everyday events provide examples. A businesswoman on a TV panel show advises young women to consider a career in computer programming. The environment is social, she explains, and working with a computer is "interactional." Résumés? Forget the old style, which read like an FBI dossier—where, when, what position—and focus on contribution. "Have you left the company better than it was when you joined it?" she asks her viewers. Men do not see career choices or résumés in such lights.

Perhaps men invented the abstract concepts of justice and equality that modern democracy is based on, but women took those concepts to mean something other than what men intended and so sought and won the vote. The "right" to education once referred only to those who could master the uniform offering of a public school. Women—mothers and teachers—took that concept to mean that every child, no matter what his limitations, deserved to be educated as far as his capacities allowed. As women find their mission in the stern religions of our past, they bend the rules more fully to the needs of their parishioners. One Episcopalian priest reaches her congregation through theater; the reaching is more important to her than the form it takes. Major issues of our day—welfare, abortion, disarmament—are profoundly feminine concepts and have been largely urged by women.

We would be crazy to plead, like Henry Higgins in *My Fair Lady*, "Why can't a woman be more like a man?" The stunning innovations women have already introduced, and the perhaps more wonderful ones yet to come, cannot happen if we hinder our children's capacity for achieving a firm gender identity by denying their need, belittling their efforts, and contradicting their choices to be clearly male or female. When a capacity itself is starved, creative ways in which it might have found expression fail to thrive. That women in our culture do not use their intelligence, aggression, and competence in the same ways as men do underlines the importance of nourishing the capacities by which both sexes generate novel solutions. We can't afford to slight either the powerful intuitions and attachments by which femininity has been traditionally expressed or the powerful abstractions and perspectives by which masculinity has been traditionally expressed. Even if it were possible to raise androgynous children, it would not be in our interest. To do so would be to lose the very richness true feminism holds out to us.

Then, too, neither sex remains the same throughout their lives. Ahead of us lie many years of study that may reveal far more about life cycles than is now known and allow us to plan for changes now barely recognized. Common observation suggests that the extraordinarily prolonged issue of separation that enables women to mother comes to its conclusion at last as their children, in turn, separate from them. The mourning, referred to these days (rather inaccurately) as the "empty nest syndrome," is real. Yet the autonomy that is wrested from loss is real, too. Women whose children have grown often exhibit a striking independence of mind and action. They may no longer become upset about a spill or a slip of the tongue that might have mortified them as younger women. They may qualify their opinions less and not need to apologize for them. And—very noticeably—they tend to take on all sorts of responsibilities beyond their homes in the larger community.

Men also change. Looking back over their years of struggle toward achievement and position, many are able to rise above the fears that plagued them in their youth. They warm up, wise up, find ways around the rat race that lead them to pleasures they had not known before. It is not unusual for a middle-aged man to reconsider his career and to alter his course somewhat. And men may become more interested in homey things, in their gardens or in cooking for family friends.

The divorce rate after a dozen or more years of marriage is high. As the children reach adolescence, the glue that has kept the couple together while they raised their children loosens, and the male and female sex roles that once seemed crucial seem so no longer. If there is a remarriage, or if the marriage survives this difficult time, the relationship often gains a new footing—more equal, more sharing, and less marked by traditional sex roles. It takes a long time, perhaps half a century, but love that truly respects the individuality of both people is finally possible.

The life cycle, and the changes in gender identity that we can observe, continues. Grandparents are not at all like parents. Coming home for a visit now, the kids may notice that their father helps prepare dinner and their mother helps him in the garden. Grandpa, who they remember as bossy and busy in their own childhoods, has a new patience with his grandchildren. Grandma, who used to be so touchy about sweets, indulges them with stacks of brownies in spite of her daughter's criticism. If we are looking for true liberation from both the competitiveness of masculinity and the compliance of femininity, we are most likely to find it in an elderly couple. These changes are brought about by aging, not by society.

The social changes that are happening now are painful, not only to those of the older generation who fear their consequences in the future, but to those of the younger generation who must endure their uncertainties in the present. As today's young men find it painful to sacrifice certain male expectations in the name of justice, so women are pained to sacrifice certain female expectations to satisfy broader goals. As Betty Friedan notes, the feminist movement failed at first to take account of how much a woman may want a baby, of how, in spite of many other ambitions, that one creeps up on her, will not let her go, forces her to recognize a commitment she did not know she had.

In the new phase of feminism Friedan envisions, men and women will seek mutuality in issues of family and child-rearing as they have begun to do in issues of self-fulfillment and contribution to the outside world. So far, we really do not know the outcomes of childrearing experiments that grew from the early years of feminism. Children of single-parent homes, of the communes of the sixties or the lesbian marriages of the seventies have not been studied in enough detail or depth, and they are not yet old enough for us to evaluate the results. We are just beginning to clarify the importance of men in children's development from infancy on, and only beginning to understand the ramifications of emotional intensity and exclusivity as it is practiced in the traditional family.

We can be sure that any change at all has outcomes. An only child is not reared in the same way as a child in a large family and turns out quite differently. Daughters of working women who mother them briefly or in a part-time fashion cannot experience continuity in the same way as a daughter who spends many years in her mother's arms and at her mother's side, nor does that mother's son have quite the same problem to resolve or the same timetable in which to resolve it. Available fathers create resources for children of both sexes that unavailable fathers cannot. Middle-aged parents have perspectives that younger parents lack, and families who manage to extend their children's relationships beyond the nuclear group invite still other differences.

As a new kind of sharing is sought by today's youth, our public institutions will become capable of functions we have not yet imagined. Men and women will exercise their capacities in forms that do not now exist. We have always been endowed with gifts that are characteristic of our genders; we must explore them now to their very depths. But in so doing, childrearing itself will drift toward unknown shores. Our only landmarks will be those we have set forth in these chapters, and other landmarks we may discover along the way. We will have to remember that males and females may do the same things—fondle a baby, march for a cause, bring home a paycheck—but they must be free to experience and express these identical endeavors in their own unique ways.

This lesson we must learn from our children. They work hard to understand their gender clearly, to express it fearlessly and in their own ways, to accept its constraints and to love its freedoms. Only by supporting their effort can we give our girls and boys the strength, the commitment, and the creativity to forge their own futures as women and men.

NOTES

Chapter 1

1. Letty Cottin Pogrebin, *Growing Up Free* (New York: McGraw-Hill, 1980), p. ix.
2. Carrie Carmichael, *Non-Sexist Childraising* (Boston: Beacon Press, 1977), p. 157.
3. Jane Lazarre, *On Loving Men* (London: Virago Press 1982), pp. 156–57.

Chapter 2

1. Eleanor E. Maccoby and Carol N. Jacklin, *The Psychology of Sex Differences* (Stanford, Calif.: Stanford University Press, 1974).

Chapter 4

1. Edward Tronick and Lauren Adamson, *Babies as People* (New York: Macmillan, 1980), p. 136.

2. Susan Goldberg and Michael Lewis. "Play Behavior in the Year Old Infant: Early Sex Differences." *Child Development* 40 (1969), 21–31.

Chapter 5

1. Evelyn Wiltshire Goodenough, "Interest in Persons as an Aspect of Sex Differences in the Early Years," *Genetic Psychology Monographs* 55 (1957), 309, cited in Maccoby and Jacklin, p. 329.

Chapter 6

1. Réné Zazzo, "Images du corps et conscience de soi." *Enfance: Psychologie, pedagogie, neuropsychiatre, sociologie* (1958), 29–43, cited in Selma Fraiberg, *Insights from the Blind* (London: Human Horizons Series, Souvenir Press, 1977), pp. 265–67.
2. "The Development of Play and Fantasy in Boys and Girls: Empirical Studies." *Psychoanalysis and Contemporary Science* 4 (1975), 529–65.

Chapter 7

1. Richard Green, *Sexual Identity Conflict in Children and Adults* (London: Duckworth, 1974).
2. A good review of studies of hormonal levels in homosexuals is Heino Meyer-Bahlburg, "Sex Hormones and Male Homosexuality in Comparative Perspective." *Archives of Sexual Behavior* 6, no. 4 (1977), 297–325 especially 300–15.
3. Jane Brody, "Some Disorders Appear Linked to Being Left-Handed," *The New York Times*, April 19, 1983, pp. C1, C10.

4. Study by Robert Stoller and Richard Green, cited in Green, *Sexual Identity Conflict in Children and Adults* (London: Duckworth, 1974), pp. 207–80.
5. Martha Kirkpatrick, Catherine Smith, and Ron Roy, "Lesbian Mothers and Their Children." *American Journal of Orthopsychiatry* 51, no. 3 (1981), 546.
6. Carmichael, *Non-Sexist Childraising* p. 47.

Chapter 8

1. Dorothy Z. Ullian, "A Developmental Study of Conceptions of Masculinity and Femininity." Unpublished dissertation, Harvard University (1976).
2. "Family Interaction Effects on Masculinity-Femininity." *Journal of Personality and Social Psychology* 8 (1968), 117–20.
3. W. E. Lambert, A. Yackley, and R. N. Hein, "Child Training Values of English Canadian and French Canadian Parents." *Canadian Journal of Behavioral Science* 3 (1971), 217–36.
4. Ullian, "A Developmental Study of Conceptions of Masculinity and Femininity," p. 169.

Chapter 9

1. Bruno Bettelheim, *Children of the Dream* (London: Thames & Hudson, 1969).
2. Pogrebin, *Growing Up Free*, p. ix.
3. Cited by E. O. Wilson, *Sociobiology: The New Synthesis* (Cambridge, Mass.: Harvard University Press, 1975), p. 170.

BIBLIOGRAPHY

BAKER, SUSAN W. "Biological Influences on Human Sex and Gender." *Signs: Journal of Women in Culture & Society* 6, no. 1 (1980): 80–96.

BARASH, DAVID. *Sociobiology and Behavior.* New York: Elsevier, 1977.

———. *The Whisperings Within: Evolution and the Origin of Human Nature.* New York: Harper & Row, 1979.

BARRY, HERBERT, MARGARET K. BACON, and IRVIN L. CHILD. "A Cross-Cultural Survey of Some Sex Differences in Socialization." *Journal of Abnormal and Social Psychology* 55 (1957): 327–32.

BEM, SANDRA L. "Gender Schema Theory: A Cognitive Account of Sex Typing." *Psychological Review* 88, no. 4 (1981): 354–64.

BENTOVIM, ARNON. "Child Development Research Findings and Psychoanalytic Theory: An Integrative Critique." In David Shaffer and Judy Dunn, eds., *The First Year of Life: Psychological and Medical Implications of Early Experience.* New York: Wiley, 1979.

BETTELHEIM, BRUNO. *Children of the Dream*. London: Thames & Hudson, 1969.

BIEBER, IRVING. *Homosexuality: A Psychoanalytic Study*. New York: Basic Books, 1962.

BOZETT, FREDERICK W. "Gay Fathers." *American Journal of Orthopsychiatry* 51, no. 3 (1981): 552–59.

CALLAGAN, ANNE R. "Gender Role and Family Relationships in Adolescent Children of Chronic Schizophrenic Mothers." *American Journal of Orthopsychiatry* 51, no. 3 (1981): 521–35.

CARMICHAEL, CARRIE. *Non-Sexist Childraising*. Boston: Beacon Press, 1977.

CHAGNON, NAPOLEON, and W. IRONS, eds. *Evolutionary Biology and Human Social Behavior*. North Scituate, Mass.: Duxbury Press, 1979.

CHODOROW, NANCY. *The Reproduction of Mothering: Psychoanalysis and the Sociology of Gender*. Berkeley: University of California Press, 1978.

CRAMER, PHEBE. "The Development of Play and Fantasy in Boys and Girls." *Psychoanalysis and Contemporary Science* 4 (1975): 529–67.

DE BEAUVOIR, SIMONE. *The Second Sex*. London: Jonathan Cape, 1963. (H. M. Pashley, trans.)

DEGLER, CARL N. *At Odds: Women and the Family in America from the Revolution to the Present*. London: Oxford University Press, 1980.

DINNERSTEIN, DOROTHY. *The Mermaid and the Minotaur: Sexual Arrangements and the Human Malaise*. New York: Harper & Row, 1976.

EHRHARDT, ANKE A., and HEINO F. L. MEYER-BAHLBURG. "Prenatal Sex Hormones and the Developing Brain." *Annual Review of Medicine* 30 (1979): 417–30.

———. "Effects of Prenatal Sex Hormones on Gender-Related Behavior." *Science* 211, no. 4488 (1981): 1312–18.

ERIKSON, ERIK H. *Childhood and Society*. London: Hogarth, 1964.

————. *Identity: Youth and Crisis*. New York: W. W. Norton, 1968.

EVANS, RAY B. "Childhood Parental Relationships of Homosexual Men." *Journal of Consulting and Clinical Psychology* 33, no. 2 (1969): 129–35.

FAGOT, BEVERLY. "Sex Differences in Toddlers' Behavior and Parental Reaction." *Developmental Psychology* 10, no. 4 (1974): 554–58.

FAST, IRENE. "Developments in Gender Identity: Gender Differentiation in Girls." *International Journal of Psycho-Analysis* 60 (1979): 443–53.

FLIEGEL, ZENIA O. "Feminine Psychosexual Development in Freudian Theory." *Psychoanalytic Quarterly* 42 (1973): 385–408.

FRAIBERG, SELMA. *The Magic Years*. London: Methuen, 1968.

————. *Insights from the Blind: Developmental Studies of Blind Children*. New York: Basic Books, 1977.

FREEDMAN, DANIEL. *Human Sociobiology: A Holistic Approach*. London: Collier Macmillan, 1979.

FRIEDAN, BETTY. *The Feminine Mystique*. London: Victor Gollanz, 1963.

FRIEDMAN, RICHARD C., and LENORE O. STERN. "Fathers, Sons, and Sexual Orientation: Replication of a Bieber Hypothesis." *Psychiatric Quarterly* 52, no. 3 (1980): 175–189.

————. "Juvenile Aggressivity and Sissiness in Homosexual and Heterosexual Males." *Journal of the American Academy of Psychoanalysis* 8, no. 3 (1980): 427–40.

GALENSON, ELEANOR, and HERMAN ROIPHE. "The Emergence of Genital Awareness During the Second Year of Life." In R. C. Friedman, R. M. Richart, and R. L. Van de Wiele, eds., *Sex Differences in Behavior*, New York: Wiley, 1974, 223–31.

————. "Some Suggested Revisions Concerning Early Female Development." *Psychoanalytic Quarterly* 24, no. 5 (1976): 29–57.

————. "The Preoedipal Development of the Boy." *Journal of the American Psychoanalytic Association* 28, no. 4 (1980): 805–27.

GILLIGAN, CAROL. "Woman's Place in Man's Life Cycle." *Harvard Educational Review* 49, no. 4 (1979): 431–46.

GOLDBERG, SUSAN, and MICHAEL LEWIS. "Play Behavior in the Year-Old Infant: Early Sex Differences." *Child Development* 40 (1969): 21–31.

GREEN, RICHARD. *Sexual Identity Conflict in Children and Adults*. New York: Basic Books, 1974.

————. "The Significance of Feminine Behaviour in Boys." *Journal of Child Psychology and Psychiatry* 16 (1975): 341–44.

————. "One-Hundred Ten Feminine and Masculine Boys: Behavioral Contrasts and Demographic Similarities." *Archives of Sexual Behavior* 5, no. 5 (1976): 425–46.

————. "Sexual Identity of 37 Children Raised by Homosexual or Transsexual Parents." *American Journal of Psychiatry* 135, no. 6 (1978): 692–97.

————. "Childhood Cross-Gender Behavior and Subsequent Sexual Preference." *American Journal of Psychiatry* 136, no. 1 (1979): 106–8.

GREIF, ESTHER BLANK. "Sex Role Playing in Pre-School Children." In Jerome S. Bruner, Alison Jolly, and Kathy Sylva, eds., *Play: Its Role in Development and Evolution*, New York: Basic Books, 1976, 385–91.

HAMBURG, DAVID A., and ELIZABETH R. McGOWN. *The Great Apes*. Menlo Park, Calif.: Benjamin/Cummings Publishing Company, 1979.

HOEFFER, BEVERLY. "Children's Acquisition of Sex-Role Behavior in Lesbian-Mother Families." *American Journal of Orthopsychiatry* 51, no. 3 (1981): 536–44.

HORNER, MATINA. "Why Bright Women Fear Success." In Carol Tavris, ed., *The Female Experience: From the Editors of Psychology Today*. Delmar, Calif.: Communications/Machines/Research, 1973, 54–57.

JACOBSON, EDITH. "Ways of Female Superego Formation and the Female Castration Conflict." *Psychoanalytic Quarterly* 45 (1976): 525–38.

JOHANSON, DONALD C., and MAITLAND A. EDEY. *Lucy: The Beginnings of Humankind.* New York: Simon & Schuster, 1981.

KAGAN, JEROME. "Sex Differences in the Human Infant." In Thomas E. McGill, Donald A. Dewsbury, and Benjamin D. Sachs, eds., *Sex and Behavior: Status and Prospectus,* New York: Plenum Press, 1978, 305–16.

KIRKPATRICK, MARTHA, CATHERINE SMITH, and RON ROY. "Lesbian Mothers and Their Children." *American Journal of Orthopsychiatry* 51, no. 3 (1981): 545–51.

KOLATA, GINA BARI. "Math and Sex: Are Girls Born with Less Ability?" *Science* 210, no. 4475 (1980): 1234–35.

KOPP, CLAIRE B., ed. *Becoming Female: Perspectives on Development.* New York: Plenum Press, 1979.

KREITLER, HANS, and SHULAMITH KREITLER. "Children's Concepts of Sexuality and Birth." *Child Development* 37 (1966): 363–78.

LANCASTER, JANE B. "Play-Mothering: The Relation Between Juvenile Females and Young Infants Among Free-Ranging Vervet Monkeys." In Jerome S. Bruner, Alison Jolly, and Kathy Sylva, eds., *Play: Its Role in Development and Evolution,* New York: Basic Books, 1976, 368–82.

LAZARRE, JANE. *On Loving Men.* London: Virago, 1982.

LEE, PATRICK C., and ROBERT S. STEWARD, eds. *Sex Differences: Cultural and Developmental Dimensions.* New York: Urizen Books, 1976.

LEIBOWITZ, LILA. *Females, Males, Families.* North Scituate, Mass.: Duxbury Press, 1976.

LLOYD, BARBARA, and JOHN ARCHER, eds. *Exploring Sex Differences.* New York: Academic Press, 1976.

LOVEJOY, C. OWEN. "The Origin of Man." *Science* 211, no. 4480 (1981): 341–50.

MACCOBY, ELEANOR E., and CAROL N. JACKLIN. *The Psychology of Sex Differences.* Stanford, Calif.: Stanford University Press, 1974.

MAHLER, MARGARET S., FRED PINE, and ANNI BERGMAN. *The Psychological Birth of the Human Infant.* New York: Basic Books, 1975.

MEAD, MARGARET. *Sex and Temperament in Three Primitive Societies.* New York: William Morrow, 1935.

————. *Male and Female.* New York: William Morrow, 1949.

MILLER, JEAN BAKER, ed. *Psychoanalysis and Women.* New York: Penguin Books, 1973.

MITCHELL, JULIET. *Psychoanalysis and Feminism.* London: Allen Lane, 1974.

MONEY, JOHN, and ANKE EHRHARDT. *Man and Woman, Boy and Girl: Differentiation and Dimorphism of Gender Identity from Conception to Maturity.* Baltimore: Johns Hopkins University Press, 1972.

MOSS, HOWARD A. "Early Sex Differences and Mother–Infant Interaction." In R. C. Friedman, R. M. Richart, and R. L. Van de Wiele, eds., *Sex Differences in Behavior,* New York: Wiley, 1974, 149–63.

NATHAN, SHARON G. "Cross-Cultural Perspectives on Penis Envy." *Psychiatry* 44 (1981): 39–44.

PIAGET, JEAN. *The Construction of Reality in the Child.* New York: Basic Books, 1954.

PINE, FRED. "On the Pathology of the Separation Individuation Process as Manifested in Later Clinical Work." *International Journal of Psycho-Analysis* 60 (1979): 225–42.

POGREBIN, LETTY COTTIN. *Growing Up Free: Raising Your Kids in the 80's.* New York: McGraw Hill, 1980.

RANSOHOFF, RITA. "An Analysis of Male Attitudes Toward Women's Cognitive Functions." *American Journal of Orthopsychiatry* 51, no. 4 (1981): 724–29.

RICH, ADRIENNE. *Of Woman Born: Motherhood as Experience and Institution.* London: Virago, 1977.

SIEGELMAN, MARVIN. "Parental Background of Male Homosexuals and Heterosexuals." *Archives of Sexual Behavior* 3,
no. 1 (1974): 3–18.

SILVERMAN, MARTIN A. "Cognitive Development and Female Psychology. *Journal of the American Psychoanalytic
Association* 29 (1981): 581–605.

SNORTUM, JOHN R., JOHN E. MARSHALL, JAMES F. GILLES-
PIE, JOHN P. MCLAUGHLIN, and LUDWIG MOSBERG. "Family Dynamics and Homosexuality." *Psychological Reports*
24 (1969): 763–70.

SOCARIDES, CHARLES W. *Beyond Sexual Freedom*. New York:
Quadrangle, 1975.

STOLLER, ROBERT J. "A Contribution to the Study of Gender
Identity: Follow-Up." *International Journal of Psycho-
Analysis* 60 (1979): 433–41.

————. *Sex and Gender*. Vol. I: *The Development of
Masculinity and Feminity*. London: Hogarth, 1969.

————. Vol. II: *The Transsexual Experiment*. London: Hogarth Press, 1972.

————. *Splitting: A Case of Female Masculinity*. London:
Hogarth Press, 1974.

TEITELBAUM, MICHAEL S., ed. *Sex Differences: Social and
Biological Perspectives*. New York: Anchor Press, 1976.

TRONICK, EDWARD, and LAUREN ADAMSON. *Babies as People*.
New York: Macmillan, 1980.

ULLIAN, DOROTHY Z. "A Developmental Study of Conceptions of Masculinity and Femininity." Unpublished
dissertation, Harvard University, 1976.

————. "Why Boys Will Be Boys: A Structural Perspective."
American Journal of Orthopsychiatry 51, no. 3 (1981): 493–
501.

WABER, DEBORAH. "Sex Differences in Mental Abilities,
Hemispheric Lateralization, and Rate of Physical Growth
at Adolescence." *Developmental Psychology* 13, no. 1
(1977): 29–38.

WHITING, BEATRICE B., and JOHN W. M. WHITING. *Chil-

dren of Six Cultures: A Psycho-Cultural Analysis. Cambridge: Harvard University Press, 1975.

WILSON, EDWARD O. *Sociobiology: The New Synthesis.* Cambridge: Harvard University Press, 1975.

———. *On Human Nature.* Cambridge: Harvard University Press, 1978.

WILSON, JAMES R., and STEVEN G. VANDENBERG. "Sex Differences in Cognition." In Thomas E. McGill, Donald A. Dewsbury, and Benjamin D. Sachs, eds., *Sex and Behavior: Status and Prospectus,* New York: Plenum Press, 1978, 317–35.

YARROW, LEON J., and MARION S. GOODWIN. "Some Conceptual Issues in the Study of Mother–Infant Interaction." *American Journal of Orthopsychiatry* 35 (1965): 473–81.

YORBURG, BETTY. *Sexual Identity and Social Change.* New York: Wiley, 1974.

INDEX